STATE V. DIAMOND

STATE V. DOYLE

Sixth Edition

STATE V. DIAMOND

STATE V. DOYLE

Sixth Edition

James H. Seckinger

NITA®

NATIONAL INSTITUTE FOR TRIAL ADVOCACY

Address inquiries to:
Reprint Permission
National Institute for Trial Advocacy
1685 38th Street, Suite 200
Boulder, CO 80301-2735
Phone: (800) 225-6482
Fax: (720) 890-7069
E-mail: permissions@nita.org

ISBN 978-1-60156-477-1 (print)
eISBN 978-1-60156-510-5 (eBook)
FBA 1477

. Wolters Kluwer

Official co-publisher of NITA.
WKLegaledu.com/NITA

Acknowledgements

This one-of-a-kind dual case file is dedicated to JoAnn Harris, a one-of-a-kind world-class teacher of advocacy. JoAnn gave so much to many students of trial advocacy through her teaching as much by example as by words; and to all the faculty who learned so much about trial advocacy, life, and the law from JoAnn; and to NITA, the organization, that benefited from her wisdom and experience in the courtroom. And finally, I will always treasure the time I was privileged to spend with JoAnn Harris, the trial lawyer and teacher who set an example for us all.

Thanks to the many lawyers who have used this file to improve their trial skills and have made valuable suggestions, and much gratitude to the students at Notre Dame Law School who have worked to make this casefile a better vehicle for learning trial skills.

To my wife, Sheila R. Block, with whom I have learned much about litigation, life, and the teaching of advocacy

J.H.S.

INTRODUCTION

State v. Diamond and *State v. Doyle* present an opportunity for a unique learning experience in the art of trial skills that cannot be duplicated in the real world:

Two persons—one man and one woman—are in an enclosed space and cannot be viewed below their shoulders; shots ring out; one person dies at the scene, the other person is charged with homicide. This case is designed to be tried twice: (1) once with the woman deceased—the man survives and is charged with homicide; (2) once with the man deceased—the woman survives and is charged with homicide.

This case file presents the same exact facts for both trials, with one exception: the gender of the defendant and the victim. This opportunity to practice trial skills will never come again.

Optimal use of this file is to try the case twice—once as *State v. Diamond* and once as *State v. Doyle*—with each student representing the State in one trial and the Defendant in the second trial.

Electronic exhibits can be found at the following website:

http://bit.ly/1P20Jea
Password: Diamond6

STATE V. DIAMOND

CONTENTS

INTRODUCTION TO STATE V. DIAMOND

A grand jury has charged Johnny Diamond with first-degree murder in the December 1, YR-1, shooting death of Trudi Doyle at the Truck Stop Café on Highway 33 outside of Nita City.

Truck Stop Café is on the outskirts of Nita City, bridging a housing development and farms—mostly small vegetable and fruit farms—and a few nurseries. A greenbelt area with some dairy and grain farms are between the Truck Stop Café, small farms, and the next town.

Ms. Doyle and Mr. Diamond had been living together for two months immediately prior to her death. Ms. Doyle was a server at the Truck Stop Café, and Mr. Diamond was a police officer with the Nita City Police Department. Both Ms. Doyle and Mr. Diamond worked night shifts.

On the morning of December 1, YR-1, Mr. Diamond, who had just resigned from the Nita City Police Department, went to the Truck Stop Café to meet Ms. Doyle, who got off work at 6:00 a.m. He sat in a booth. Ms. Doyle was sitting in a booth at the other side of the restaurant talking with the other servers. She did not speak to Mr. Diamond, and then at 6:30 a.m., Ms. Doyle got up from the booth and went to the entranceway of the café. Mr. Diamond followed her, and they talked for a few minutes. Two shots rang out. Ms. Doyle slumped to the floor and died within minutes. Mr. Diamond remained at the scene and was arrested when the police arrived.

The applicable law is contained in the statutes and the proposed jury instructions set forth at the end of the file.

All years in these materials are stated in the following form:

YR-0   indicates the current, actual year in which the students are trying the case (e.g., please use "2016," not "YR-0" when presenting the case);

YR-1   indicates the previous year (e.g., 2015, if 2016 is the current year);

YR-2   indicates the second preceding year, etc. (e.g., 2014, if 2016 is the current year).

INSTRUCTIONS FOR USE AS A FULL TRIAL

When this case file is used for a full trial, the following witnesses are available. Diamond is male and Doyle is female; every other witness may be male or female. **Each witness' first name is determined by the gender of the person playing the witness role.**

State: E. A. Benbrook

Joseph/JoAnn Foster

Beth/Brian Kelly

Dr. Jamie Pierce

Defense: Johnny Diamond, accused [must be called in a mock trial]

Eric/Estelle Mason

Jeanne/John Madden

Each party must call *two* witnesses to testify.

Each party may petition the court for the admission of facts from a witness not called. The moving party must show that the fact(s) would be admissible if the witness were called to testify and the need.

REQUIRED STIPULATIONS

1. The facts in the Introduction are agreed facts and admissible without further proof.

2. Neutron activation tests of Johnny Diamond's hands were positive

3. Neutron activation tests of Trudi Doyle's hands were negative.

4. Test of powder burns on Trudi Doyle's jacket were inconclusive due to extensive bleeding.

5. Blood on the jacket was type O negative. Trudi Doyle has type O negative blood.

6. Comparison of the bullet found in Trudi Doyle's body with a bullet fired from Diamond's gun show that both were fired from that gun.

7. The gun was examined for fingerprints, but no usable prints were found.

8. The gun has a trigger pull of six pounds. This is an average pull, midway between a hair trigger and a heavy trigger pull.

9. When fired, the gun recoils approximately 15 degrees.

10. The Memorial Hospital medical records were made and kept in the regular course of the hospital's business. William Coleman, the medical records librarian, would so testify if called as a witness.

11. The transcript of the statement given by Johnny Diamond is authentic.

12. The Beretta 84FS Cheetah in the photograph is the pistol Sergeant Benbrook retrieved from the Truck Stop Café on December 1, YR-1.

13. Johnny Diamond has owned the pistol pictured in the photograph ever since he bought it while serving in the military.

IN THE CIRCUIT COURT OF
DARROW COUNTY, NITA

THE PEOPLE OF THE STATE OF NITA	)	
	)	
v.	)	Case No. CR2216
	)	
JOHN DIAMOND,	)	INDICTMENT
Defendant.	)	

The Grand Jury in and for the county of Darrow, State of Nita, upon their oath and in the name and by the authority of the State of Nita, does hereby charge the following offense under the Criminal Code of the State of Nita:

That on December 1, YR-1, at and within the County of Darrow in the State of Nita, John Diamond committed the crime of

MURDER IN THE FIRST DEGREE

In violation of Section 18-3-102 of the Nita Criminal Code of 1974, as amended, in that he, after deliberation and with the intent to cause the death of a person other than himself, caused the death of Trudi Doyle with a deadly weapon, namely a Beretta semi-automatic pistol.

Contrary to the form of the Statute and against the peace and dignity of the People of the State of Nita.

A TRUE BILL:

Jeanne Mitchell

Jeanne Mitchell
Foreperson of the Grand Jury

M.P. Mickers

M. P. Mickers
District Attorney Darrow County
State of Nita 99995
(828) 555-3884

DATED: December 15, YR-1

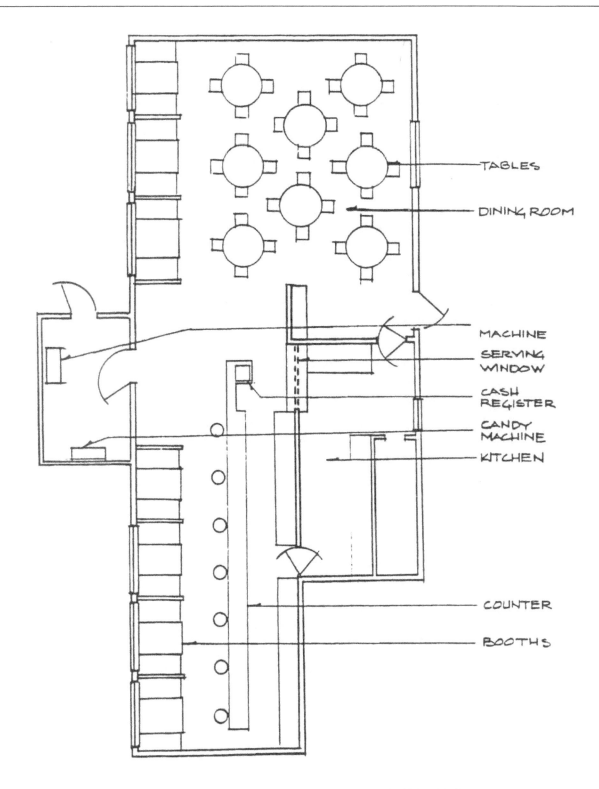

TABLES

DINING ROOM

MACHINE

SERVING
WINDOW

CASH
REGISTER

CANDY
MACHINE

KITCHEN

COUNTER

BOOTHS

DIAGRAM OF TRUCK STOP CAFE
HIGHWAY 33, NITA CITY

(NOT DRAWN TO SCALE)

NITA CITY POLICE DEPARTMENT

OFFENSE REPORT

Re: Trudi Doyle
Location: The Truck Stop Café
                 Highway 33
                 Nita City, Nita
Offense: Homicide
Date of Report: December 9, YR-1
By: Sgt. E. A. Benbrook
                 Homicide Division

On December 1, YR-1, at about 6:55 a.m., I received a telephone call that there had been a shooting at the Truck Stop Café. I went immediately to the café. When I arrived, I met Officers Johnson and White, who also had just arrived. I instructed Officers Johnson and White to secure the scene and check for witnesses in the restaurant.

On checking the scene, I saw Trudi Doyle lying in the entranceway of the café, and Johnny Diamond was kneeling next to her, holding her hand. A handgun was by his side. There was blood on the front of her jacket, and Doyle appeared to be dead—her eyes were open, but she didn't move at all. I didn't touch the body or check to determine if Doyle was, in fact, dead.

After seeing Ms. Doyle lying there and Mr. Diamond kneeling next to her, I picked up the gun and said to Mr. Diamond, "All right, Diamond, what happened?" He didn't say anything; he just kind of stared off into space. I said, "Let's go," or something like that, and then Mr. Diamond got up. I took him to the police car, handcuffed him, and placed him in the back of the car. I told him that he was under arrest for investigation of assault, or homicide if Doyle was dead, and advised Diamond of his Miranda rights—to remain silent and to have a lawyer. (I read the rights off of our departmental card that we carry.) Diamond didn't say anything or respond at all. He just calmly sat there in the car. He looked normal and appeared to understand and know everything that was going on. I then left the car and instructed Officer White to stand at the rear of the car while I continued the investigation.

The coroner arrived and pronounced Trudi Doyle dead. Her body was transferred to the County Morgue for an autopsy by Deputy Coroner Dr. Pierce.

Ms. Doyle was found lying in the entranceway to the Truck Stop Café. It is a glass-enclosed structure nine feet wide by twelve feet long (inside measurements). The lower four feet of the walls are wood, and the rest is glass. Both doors are glass. I found a package of gum (unopened) on the floor next to Ms. Doyle. The package was a box the shape of a deck of cards only thinner, and the gum was in foil that slides out of the box. I first saw it when Ms. Doyle's body was being moved out of the entranceway. The package was partially covered by Ms. Doyle's legs. There was no blood on it. Two expended cartridges were found in the northeast corner of the entranceway.

A mutilated bullet was lodged in the west wall fourteen inches to the south of the vending machine, thirty inches above the floor. I marked the cartridges with my initials, placed the cartridges and the package of gum in an evidence envelope, and then placed the envelope in an evidence locker at the station.

I spoke with Beth Kelly, who was identified by Officer Johnson as an eyewitness. Kelly told me that Ms. Doyle had gone to get gum and Mr. Diamond had intercepted her in the entranceway, that Kelly saw Ms. Doyle shake her heard "no," Mr. Diamond nod his head "yes," then two shots rang out, and Ms. Doyle slumped to the floor. At that time I didn't speak with the other two witnesses, Eric Mason (a server) and Joseph Foster (a local farmer), but simply got their names and addresses.

I checked on Mr. Diamond in the car once or twice during my investigation at the scene, and each time he was still calmly sitting in the car. I never saw him look over at Ms. Doyle, not even when the coroner came and examined Ms. Doyle. After the coroner examined Ms. Doyle, I told Mr. Diamond that Doyle was dead. He didn't respond at all, just calmly sat there like nothing had happened.

Officers Johnson and White took Mr. Diamond to the county jail, and he was booked for investigation of homicide. As part of the booking process, Mr. Diamond was tested for drugs and alcohol. This took place at approximately 1:00 p.m. These tests came back negative. After the booking process, the lab performed a neutron activation test of Mr. Diamond's hands. The results were positive. The lab also performed a neutron activation test of Trudi Doyle's hands at the morgue. Results negative.

I retained custody of the handgun that I found next to Mr. Diamond and the body of Trudi Doyle. It was a Beretta Cheetah, a .380 caliber semi-automatic pistol, serial number D 08865. When I got back to the police department, I put my initials on the gun and placed it in an evidence locker. The evidence locker is in our custodian's office. I completed the forms for the custodian. There is always a person on duty at this office, and there is a ledger or receipt for signing articles in and out. That way we have a record of where things are at all times.

Mr. Diamond gave a statement on the day of the shooting, December 1, at approximately 3:30 p.m. The statement was given in the presence of me, Officer James Anderson, and Megan Schmidt, a certified shorthand reporter.

On December 2, I checked out gun registration files and determined that the pistol had been registered to Johnny Diamond in November of YR-2. All guns have to be registered, and records are kept in the police department with a central file for the state in Capitol City.

I then examined and test fired the pistol. The gun was operable. I test fired it into a special box designed for that purpose and then recovered the bullet. I had received a bullet from Dr. Pierce, deputy coroner, that had been recovered from the body of Ms. Doyle. I compared the two bullets by examining them under a microscope and looking at the "lands" and "grooves."

There were identical markings on both of the bullets, indicating they had been fired by the same gun. In order to be absolutely certain, I sent the bullets to the Nita State Crime Laboratory and requested their opinion. I received the bullets back with a letter, signed by Mr. Michael J. Harvey, stating that he had examined them, that they had identical markings, and it was his opinion that they had been fired from the same gun. The bullet that had been recovered from the entranceway wall was too mutilated to permit comparison.

I received special training in firearm testing and identification at the Nita State Crime Laboratory in Capitol City. This was about two years ago. I keep up-to-date on it by reading the material distributed by the Nita State Crime Laboratory and the FBI.

I submitted the jacket Doyle was wearing to the State Crime Laboratory for testing. Results for powder burns were inconclusive due to the amount of blood on the jacket. Blood type same as Doyle's. Shape of the two holes in the front of the jacket indicated that the holes were caused by bullets.

I knew Johnny Diamond when he was a police officer with our department. He was thirty years old, and a big man, over six feet tall and around 200 pounds. I first met Johnny in November YR-2, when he joined the force. I knew him fairly well, although I never worked with him. I would see him at the station quite often, and we talked about general topics. I found him pleasantly talkative, but not very revealing about his personal life. He did mention that he was married with two children, but that he has been separated from them for some time and was in the process of getting a divorce. He talked about his children a little, but never about his ex-wife. He dated some girls occasionally, but I guess they broke off the relationships. Then he met Trudi Doyle. He would talk about her, although never with any specifics. The conversation would always be general and just enough for me to know that he was with her. I knew Ms. Doyle, but only to recognize her and know that she worked as a server at the Truck Stop Café. I didn't know anything about her personal life.

On the day Trudi Doyle was shot, December 1, I was at the station and saw Johnny Diamond. He came off duty from his shift at 5:30 a.m. I saw him as he came into the station, and he went back to his locker. As he was leaving I saw him, and we talked for a few minutes. He said that he had just resigned and that he was going to California to start over. I wished him good luck and kidded him about his love life. He said, "Well, wish me luck on that; I'm going to talk to her." I don't remember the exact words, but that was basically what he said.

When I was talking to him, I noticed that he had his "off-duty" gun in his shoulder holster. A shoulder holster fits under your jacket, so it is an easy way for a cop to carry his firearm when out of his uniform. I did notice that he never clipped the gun into the holster; I just assumed he did this so he could pull it out at a moment's notice. Johnny's shoulder holster was under his left arm, meaning he would reach it with his right hand. I saw that the hammer was back, and it was in the cocked position. I just assumed the safety was on, but I couldn't see it. It would be extremely hazardous to carry the gun cocked if the safety is off. I don't think it is unusual to carry a gun cocked with a round in the chamber, as long as the safety is on, especially for a police officer. He zipped up his jacket and left.

I talked to Diamond around 6:00 a.m. I got the call from the Truck Stop Café about the shooting around 6:50 a.m.

Submitted by:

Sgt. E.A. Benbrook
Sgt. E.A. Benbrook*
Homicide Division
Nita City Police Department

---

* Sgt. E. A. Benbrook has been a police officer with the Nita City Police Department for twelve years. He has been a sergeant for four years and has been in charge of the homicide division for two years. He is married with two children.

Nita City Police Department

Statement of Beth/Brian Kelly

My name is Beth Kelly. I am a short-order cook at the Truck Stop Café, working the day shift from 6:00 a.m. until 2:30 p.m. I live at 405½ South Fourth Street, Nita City. I am twenty-six, single, and live by myself.

I knew Trudi Doyle because she worked at the Truck Stop Café with me. She also lived in a spare room in my apartment for about six months. I also know Johnny Diamond. He used to come into the Truck Stop Café a lot, and then he began dating Trudi. Trudi was thirty-one years old and had been working as a server at the Truck Stop Café since sometime in March YR-1. She was married and had a little boy, but last I heard she was in the process of divorcing her husband. She'd been separated from her husband since she came to Nita City and began working in the café. Johnny Diamond is in his late twenties, I think. He is married with two children, but is separated from his wife and children. Trudi told me that his divorce has been pending for some time.

On December 1, YR-1, I arrived at work on time, as usual. In fact, I always arrive between 5:30 and 5:45 a.m. When I walked in, I saw Trudi Doyle and two or three other servers who were coming off their shift. They went to a booth on the north side of the café and had some coffee. After a little while, I got my first order of the day, hotcakes. I remember this because when I went to the serving window to get an order, I could see Trudi get up from the booth and walk toward the front door. I turned back around and saw that she had gotten some gum from the machine and that Diamond was also standing in the entranceway, but with his back to the door. He was blocking her way back into the café. He must have been sitting in a back booth because I didn't see him get up and walk to the front.

Trudi was facing me, and Diamond was in front of her with his back toward me. Trudi had a pack of gum shaped like a box in her left hand. It was a blue and white package, the size of a deck of cards only thinner, and the gum was in a foil packet that pulls out. She had quit smoking and was using gum to keep off the cigarettes. Trudi would always go the entranceway to get candy or gum from the vending machine there.

It looked like they were about to have a fight, if you know what I mean, from the way Diamond sort of stepped in front of her to block her path to the door and by the way she shook her head "no" when he asked her something. I couldn't hear what was being said since they were in the entranceway, but I did see her shake her head "no," and he nodded his head "yes." I could see pretty well because the entranceway is glass-enclosed, and also the door is all glass. I was only fifteen feet or so away from them, the serving window being six to eight feet behind the cash register. The next thing I knew I heard two bangs; they were shots, quick like firecrackers. I heard shouts, and I thought, "Oh, God, someone's been shot." I started for the back so I could call the police.

By the time I came out to the front of the café, Trudi was lying on the floor, and Mr. Diamond was kneeling next to her holding her hand. I grabbed a wet rag from out front and went back to help revive the dishwasher. When I came back to the front of the café the police had come, and they took Mr. Diamond to the police car. I talked to Sgt. Benbrook and told him what I saw.

I had seen Diamond in the café before and knew it was him as soon as I saw him that morning on December 1. He usually came in early to have breakfast and pick up Trudi as she came off her shift.

Trudi was right-handed. I often saw her writing the orders and checks for the customers.

We were pretty good friends, and she was good company for me. Trudi had a pretty tough life, and I felt for her. Trudi grew up in a small town a little ways from Nita City. She was the youngest of four kids, and her parents were pretty poor. I guess she did really good at school, but couldn't afford to go to college, so she joined the Army after high school. She sometimes hinted that something else happened during that time, but she never told me what it was. I figured some guy broke her heart, but I don't know.

Trudi was in the Army for four years, and she used to talk a lot about the training she received there. I guess she was one of the best shots with small arms, like pistols. She always said the rifles were too big for her, but the pistols were just her size; like Annie Oakley meets Goldilocks, I guess. She never got a chance to see combat, only did clerical work in an office on the base. She said that she used to go to the shooting range twice as often as she was supposed to. She was real comfortable around guns and used to joke around a lot about them. Honestly, it sometimes made me a little nervous. I was just glad she didn't have a gun when she was living with me.

After her time in the Army, she married a guy she met on the base, and I guess it didn't go well from the start. He was a drunk and used to hit her all the time. She left him and moved to Nita City a couple years ago. She had one child, a boy around four, and she talked about him often. He is living with Trudi's mom in Capitol City, and the kid sometimes visits his dad. I guess her ex was making the divorce real ugly, fighting for custody and all of that. She worried a lot about these problems. In fact, she suffered from some pretty serious depression. When she was staying with me, I used to hear her crying in her room pretty often. I knocked a few times to see if I could help, but she never answered.

Diamond wanted to go out West, and he really wanted Trudi to go with him. But she couldn't make up her mind, and she seemed reluctant. We talked about it four or five times the last two or three days. She liked Diamond, but she didn't know if she wanted to settle down again so soon. It would be easier if he just stayed in town. She was worried about getting into another bad relationship, especially with a cop. She said that she thought she loved Diamond, but wasn't sure.

The first time I saw them together in the café that morning was when they were in the entranceway. Trudi had been sitting with the other servers before she got up to get the gum. Diamond must have been sitting someplace else by himself. She did not go talk to him—he went after her.

There were about ten to fifteen people in the café when Trudi was shot. There were a few people at the counter and some in the booths. I really don't want to talk about this anymore.

I have read the above statement consisting of three pages, and it is true and correct.

Signed: *Beth Kelly*   Date: 12/4/YR-1
            Beth Kelly

Witness: *E.A. Benbrook*   Date: 12/4/YR-1
            Sgt. E.A. Benbrook

NITA CITY POLICE DEPARTMENT

STATEMENT OF JOSEPH/JOANN FOSTER*

My name is Joseph Foster. My spouse and I run an organic farm on the outskirts of Nita City. Three or four times a week I drive my truck into town for supplies. I also come into town to run my stand at the farmer's market every Thursday. Either way, I head into town after my early morning chores and usually stop at the Truck Stop Café for breakfast. On December 1, YR-1, the day of the shooting, I had done just that and entered the café at about 6:15 or 6:20 a.m. I sat at the counter, and Mason waited on me, as usual. I ordered my hotcakes and orange juice like I do every time I'm there. I was sitting at the counter, one seat over from the cash register.

I don't know any of the other servers by name, but I noticed a group of them—three or four—sitting in a booth, far to my left, when I first walked in. The place wasn't very crowded yet, and I guess they were taking a coffee break, till business picked up.

After ordering, I just sat there making conversation with Mason, who was busy cleaning up the counter where I was sitting. Several seconds went by, and then Johnny Diamond came tearing down the aisle to my right. He must've been sitting at one of the booths in that area of the restaurant, but I hadn't noticed him till then. He seemed to be in a big hurry and walked right past me to the front door, which I had my back to. Being curious, I tried to listen to what made Johnny pass by without saying hello. After I heard the door open, I heard what sounded like the vending machine ejecting candy or a pack of gum. I recognized that sound because I get a candy bar or a pack of gum every Monday; my spouse is trying to get me to quit smoking, so I substitute candy or gum. Can't smoke anywhere these days so might as well quit. After Johnny went into the entranceway and the glass door shut behind him, I could hear him talking to a woman, but I couldn't make out what they were saying through the door—plus it wasn't really my business. I started to say something to Mason when I heard a shot fired in the entranceway. I immediately hit the floor to my right as my combat instincts told me; I had fought in Afghanistan, and I've been spooky about sounds ever since.

---

* This statement was given to Sgt. Benbrook at Foster's farm on December 3, YR-1.

Then another shot rang out. From my military background, I'd estimate it was five seconds before the second shot was fired.

I am legally blind in my left eye and have very poor vision in the right one. I lost my vision in a training accident after my service in Afghanistan. I was training some new recruits in the use of riot grenades (flash bangs), and one of the recruits dropped his grenade in the pit. The flash damaged my right eye, and some shrapnel from the casing found its way into my left eye, permanently blinding it. I was medically discharged from the Army after the grenade incident and have lived a peaceful life away from guns since my discharge. In fact, the shooting was the first time I had been near gunfire since my discharge. One nice side effect of my vision loss was that over time my other senses were heightened as I became less dependent on my eyes. This is a mixed blessing, because the coffee at the Truck Stop Café is horrible, but the pancakes are fantastic.

During my service in Afghanistan, I was a NCO in the Special Forces, with specialized training in nighttime infiltration. This training focused on the ability to judge the distance and number of troops in a patrol by the sounds they made moving through the terrain. By measuring the time in between sounds a soldier can easily know the patrol's speed, composition, and direction of travel.*

When I was sure all the shooting was finished, I got back on my feet and told Mason to call 911. I made my way over to the entranceway, but there were other people around, and I didn't want to get in the way. The people at the café said the woman was Trudi Doyle and the guy was Johnny Diamond. I'll never forget that day.

I have known Johnny Diamond for a number of years. He is a regular at my booth at the farmer's market. He always buys a couple heads of lettuce and whatever beef I have on special. Lately he has also taken to buying some flowers. I gibed him the first time he bought flowers, saying he was going soft. I remember this because my spouse told me to shut it and leave the nice young man alone. Diamond responded that he had found a good reason to go soft and was even thinking about leaving the force. I told him not to get married, but just to run off with the girl; of course my spouse hit me with some celery for that one. The last time he came to the booth, he didn't buy anything, said he was

---

* Assume that women now serve in the Special Forces, both in training and in the field, so Foster may be male or female.

leaving town and gonna take his girl with him. I wished him the best and tried to sell him some jerky for the road. I never did meet his girlfriend.

I remember all this very distinctly. After all it was the biggest thing that had happened to me in years, being an eyewitness, or I guess more of an earwitness, to a killing, that is. I'm not about to forget the details of such an experience.

I have read the above statement consisting of two pages, and it is true and correct.

Signed: *Joseph Foster*   Date: 12/3/YR-1
                           Joseph Foster

Witness: *E.A. Benbrook*   Date: 12/3/YR-1
                           Sgt. E.A. Benbrook

NITA CITY POLICE DEPARTMENT

STATEMENT OF ERIC/ESTELLE MASON*

My name is Eric Mason. I am a server at the Truck Stop Café, and I live at 502 North Allen, Nita City. I am thirty-nine years old and single. I work the day shift at the Truck Stop Café. I was there the day Trudi Doyle died.

I begin work at 6:00 a.m., which is the time the night shift ends, and my duties include waiting on customers seated at the counter. On the morning of December 1, YR-1, I arrived on time and waited on my first customer at about 6:15. The customer was Joseph Foster, a farmer who comes in several times a week around this time. I took Foster's order for hotcakes and coffee, Foster's usual. There weren't too many people in the café at that time. Foster and one other person were seated at the counter, and there were two or three booths that had people. Foster was sitting at the counter, one seat over from the cash register.

I distinctly remember seeing Officer Diamond seated at a booth not far from the counter. He came in often to pick up a server, Trudi Doyle, when her shift was over, so I thought nothing of seeing him seated there.

A little while after I had taken Foster's order (I don't know exactly what time), I saw Officer Diamond hurry past the counter toward the front door. I remember this because he was moving so quickly. I was wiping the counter area near Foster at the time, but looked up to see where Officer Diamond was going so fast. He went through the door to the entranceway where Trudi was at the vending machine. It looked like she had gotten a pack of gum or some candy. She had turned from the vending machine and was facing inside. I couldn't hear what was being said, but I could see that they were talking and that Trudi was shaking her head "no" and Officer Diamond was nodding "yes." I could see Officer Diamond was standing in the doorway. The next thing I knew, Trudi moved toward Diamond, and she made a quick movement. Diamond moved towards her quickly and kind of with a jerk. That's all I could see because his back was to me. Then I heard the sound of

---

* This statement was given to Sgt. Benbrook at the Truck Stop Café on December 5, YR-1.

a shot and a few seconds later, another one. The shots were close to one another, about one to three seconds apart. I heard Office Diamond and Trudi shout, saw her on the floor, and realized she had been shot. Foster had jumped off the seat and laid flat on the ground, I guess, when Foster heard the shots. When Foster jumped back up, Foster told me to call 911.

I immediately went to the kitchen for help and learned that someone had already called the police. When I returned to the front of the café, Officer Diamond was kneeling over Trudi Doyle, holding her hand.

The whole incident happened very fast, maybe within twenty or thirty seconds from the time I saw Officer Diamond rush past me, but it is difficult to figure such timing. I was standing only eight or ten feet from the entranceway where it happened.

I didn't see Officer Diamond's hands. I could only see his back and the upper part of Trudi's body: her head and shoulders. Officer Diamond was standing in front of her. The lower part of the entranceway is wood for about three or four feet up from the floor. Above that it's all glass.

I didn't know Trudi real well because our shifts were different, but I would talk to her most days when I was coming and she was leaving. A couple of days before the shooting, I saw her do a strange thing. She was drinking coffee and waiting for her ride after her shift, and I saw her pour something into her coffee from a small bottle. I couldn't see what it was, but she did it under the table like she was trying to be sneaky or something.

I know a lot of people think Officer Diamond is a great guy, but Diamond has always been a jerk to me. He once pulled me over because my taillight was out. I thought it would be no big deal and told him I would fix it when I could. He pulls me out of the car and makes me do all these tests like I had been drinking. I am a recovering alcoholic and haven't had a drink in three years and told him so. He wouldn't have anything to do with it. Told me people never change and once a drunk always a drunk. After I passed all his tests, he still made me blow in the stupid breathalyzer thing. Finally he let me get back in my car, but made me sit there while he ran my insurance and driver's license. Then after all of that, he still gave me a ticket for the broken taillight. The only reason I could ever figure he was mean to me was earlier that day when he had come to pick up Trudi, she and I were chatting and joking when he came in. He looked at me like he wanted to punch me just for making her laugh. He didn't say anything at the time, just grabbed Trudi's hand, and they left even though she was protesting that she wanted to hear the end of my joke.

I don't know if you are going to talk to that nutter Foster, but I should tell you Foster's crazy as a March hare. Foster's got some tall tales about being in the Army Special Forces or something, but I heard from someone way back that Foster was a supply sergeant in some back area. Who knows what's true, but I just always take what Foster says with a grain of salt. If you ask my opinion Foster's getting to the point where Foster doesn't know the truth from fiction.

I should probably tell you this, too, now that I'm thinking about it. The day before Trudi Doyle was shot, a few days after my run in with Officer Diamond over my broken taillight, Trudi came to apologize to me. Seems Officer Diamond had told her about pulling me over, and she had told him off. Trudi looked just furious when she was telling me this, shaking her fists and swearing. Trudi said she gets so mad when he gets like that, she could just kill him. I don't think she meant it; just blowing off steam.

I have read the above, and it is my statement.

Signed: *Eric Mason*   Date: 12/5/YR-1
Eric Mason

Witness: *E.A. Benbrook*   Date: 12/5/YR-1
Sgt. E.A. Benbrook

STATEMENT OF JEANNE/JOHN MADDEN*

My name is Jeanne Madden. I am a police officer in Nita City. I am thirty-two, married, with three children, and live at 481 Olive Street, Nita City. I have been a member of the Nita City Police Department for a little over nine years. I was born and raised in Nita City. I worked in my father's hardware store for a few years after high school before entering the Nita Police Academy at age twenty-two. After successfully completing police training, I became a member of the Nita City Police Department and worked my way up through the ranks until reaching my present position of sergeant.

Johnny Diamond is thirty and also lived in Nita City all his life. Although I never met Johnny until he joined the police force last year, I knew who he was, as he and my brother were about the same age and went to high school together. I, at that time, knew little about Johnny except for the fact that he had never had any police trouble.

Johnny Diamond became a member of the Nita City Police Department in November YR-2, after just having completed four years in the Marines and the usual police training. While in the Marines, he had become an expert in the use of firearms and owned a Beretta Cheetah semi-automatic pistol that he always carried while off duty.

Johnny Diamond attained a commendable record during his short time as a police officer. I was personally aware of his performance and progress since I was responsible for filing detailed quarterly reports on him. Johnny Diamond was competent in all aspects of police work and displayed a good attitude toward his work.

In Nita City, we encourage, but do not require, all police officers to carry a loaded firearm while off duty. This is written right in the Nita City Police Department Duty Manual. Carrying the weapon in this way enables officers to better carry out their sworn affirmative duty to enforce the law twenty-four hours a day. It has been our experience that unarmed, off-duty officers are sometimes unable to effectively fulfill that duty when faced with certain emergency situations.

---

* This statement was given to John DeGroff, investigator for defense counsel, at Madden's home on December 6, YR-1.

It is my understanding that Officer Diamond was carrying his off-duty weapon immediately after having resigned from the force on December 1 and that this instrument caused the death of Trudi Doyle less than an hour after he went off duty that day.

I am familiar with the Cheetah semi-automatic. Several of our officers have such a weapon; also I'm used to carrying that kind of gun myself. It was my practice to carry the gun with the hammer in the uncocked position with a bullet in the firing chamber. In my opinion, this is the best way for a police officer to carry this gun because with a round in the chamber it is ready to be used in case of an emergency. It is also very safe because the safety is on, and there is little chance the gun will go off accidentally.

Johnny Diamond and I both worked the night shift (9:00 p.m. to 5:30 a.m.). As I was responsible for familiarizing the new officers with their duties, Johnny Diamond and I occasionally worked together on an assignment or patrol beat. We became friendly with one another, but not to the extent where we socialized outside of work. Also, our outside interests were perhaps divergent, as I am married with three children, and he is separated from his wife.

Having worked with Diamond for several months, I got to know him quite well, both professionally and personally. He was a good officer and an excellent person to work with. Occasionally we would talk about our personal lives, and I knew that he was married with two children, but he had been separated from his wife and children. His divorce had been pending since January YR-1. He began dating Trudi Doyle sometime in late September YR-1, and they had lived together for a couple of months before Trudi's death on December 1, YR-1. Diamond seemed so much happier after he met Trudi Doyle. He was excited about life and looking forward to the future. Although I didn't personally know Ms. Doyle, I had seen her a couple of times at the Truck Stop Café, where she worked as a server. That particular diner was a favorite coffee-break spot for several police officers.

During the night of November 27, YR-1 (four days before Doyle was shot), Diamond and I were on patrol duty together. It was at that time that Diamond first told me of his decision to resign from the police force and move to California. Diamond said that he loved Trudi and wanted to take her to California with him because of her dissatisfaction with Nita City and her depressed state of mind. Diamond then told me about what had happened with Trudi just a day or so before. Apparently Trudi had attempted to commit suicide by taking an overdose of barbiturates and that Diamond arrived home just in time to save her life by inducing vomiting and taking her to the hospital. Diamond also told me that she at one other time had unsuccessfully attempted suicide with aspirin.

After Trudi's latest suicide attempt, Diamond said that he got really worried about Trudi and knew he had to shock her into reality in order to cure her of her inclination to kill herself. To impress on Trudi the seriousness of her act, Diamond pointed to his unloaded pistol and said, "If anyone is going to kill you, I am." This happened the afternoon that Diamond took Trudi home from the hospital. Diamond was very worried about Trudi's depressed condition, and he thought maybe that would shock her out of it and make her realize the seriousness and stark reality of her suicide attempts.

Diamond also told me that Trudi had not yet made up her mind to go to California with him, but that he would leave with or without her because he wanted to get away from life in Nita City.

After his shift ended that night (morning of November 28), Diamond submitted his resignation to become effective December 1, YR-1.

On the day of December 1, Diamond completed his normal shift at 5:30 a.m., and he left his forwarding address with the desk clerk, so his paycheck would be sent to him. Ms. Doyle was shot in the Truck Stop Café at around 6:30 a.m. that morning, but I know little more than that both Diamond and Doyle were present at the scene of the shooting when the police arrived and that Diamond did not resist arrest. I was at home and asleep at the time of the shooting.

I would like to go on the record again as stating that Johnny was a fine officer of the law and had received several commendations for superior duty. I have read the above, and it is my statement.

Signed: *J. Madden*   Date: 12/6/YR-1
            Sgt. J. Madden

Witness: **John DeGroff**   Date: 12/6/YR-1
            John DeGroff

NITA CITY POLICE DEPARTMENT

STATEMENT OF JOHN DIAMOND*

This statement was given by John Diamond at the Nita City Police Station between 3:30 and 4:00 p.m. on December 1, YR-1. The statement was transcribed stenographically in the presence of Sgt. E. A. Benbrook, Officer James Anderson, and the shorthand reporter, Megan Schmidt.

By Diamond:

Yes, I know I've been charged with the first-degree murder of my girlfriend, Trudi Doyle.

I grew up in Nita City, left when I was twenty-one in June of YR-10, and came back in October YR-2 (when I was twenty-nine). I was born March, YR-31. I am thirty years old, married with two children, but have been separated from my wife since August YR-2. My wife has the children, and her divorce action has been pending since January YR-1.

I met Trudi shortly after arriving in Nita City in October YR-2. Trudi was twenty-six years old when we met; Trudi's birthday is October 18, YR-28. She was married; had one child, a boy; and had been divorced since June YR-2.

I was a police officer with the Nita City Police Department from November YR-2 to December YR-1. Before that, I had been in the Marines for eight years (June YR-10 to July YR-2), and before that, I had a couple of jobs right out of high school that went nowhere (June YR-13 to May YR-10). I had no particular career goals, just coasting along, and finally got it together and decided to enlist in the Marines (June YR-10). The Marines really helped to straighten me out in that respect. I got an Honorable Discharge and was awarded a Purple Heart while fighting in Afghanistan.

Trudi and I began dating in late September YR-1, about two months before her death. Trudi was a server at the Truck Stop Café, a highway truck stop on the edge of Nita City; Trudi worked the night

---

shift, like I did, so we had a lot of time to spend with each other during the day. I soon found myself falling in love with Trudi. I asked her to marry me as soon as our respective divorces were final. She said she loved me, too, but I could never be certain about Trudi's feelings because she was moody and often depressed.

We lived together at my place for about a month before December 1. I knew a lot about judo from my days as a Marine, and so I spent time teaching Trudi to defend herself and how to disarm an assailant. Trudi seemed to really enjoy these lessons, treating them like games. She particularly enjoyed trying to snatch my gun from my holster whenever I was armed in her presence. Because of this, I always removed all the bullets from my pistol when around Trudi so it wouldn't accidentally discharge. I constantly carried a gun, whether on or off duty, since police officers in Nita City are encouraged, though not required, to do so in order that we might not be helpless in an emergency situation. I had a .380 Beretta Cheetah, and when off duty, I carried either it or my service pistol.

Trudi had a lot of experience with guns herself. Trudi was in the Army before she got married, and she was quite skilled—a markswoman, I guess. Trudi received training in the Army on the Beretta 92fs semi-automatic pistol. The Cheetah is the smaller version of that standard-issue pistol. After we had been dating for a while, I gave her the Cheetah as a present. She was real excited about it and used it when we would go shooting together.

The reason for the judo was Trudi's fear of some truck drivers and salesmen she met daily on her job. She was a small woman, and she was particularly afraid of one truck driver who used vulgar language and made several passes at her. That's another reason I gave her the pistol. I wanted to be sure she could protect herself against punks like that.

It really upset me how sad Trudi was all the time. She had a pretty tough childhood. Trudi's dad was in and out of work, and they never had any money. Trudi talked a lot about how different her life would have been if she could have gone to college. Instead, she joined the Army, and that's where she met her husband, but he had been nothing but trouble for her. From the time I met Trudi, she was up and down with depression—when not depressed, Trudi was a joy to be with and had a bright future, but when depressed, life was a real struggle for her.

In fact, Trudi tried to kill herself twice. The first time was before I met her. She had taken a large amount of aspirin, but only got sick and had a "ringing" sensation in her ears. I found out about this only because of her second attempt on her life, which occurred on November 26, about a week ago. I came home that afternoon to find that Trudi had taken an overdose of sleeping pills. I force-fed her milk and olive oil, then made her vomit to get rid of the pills and rushed her to the hospital. They pumped her stomach and held her overnight for observation.

I usually worked the night shift, but November 26 was my day off, so I didn't have to go on duty that night. I stayed at the hospital with Trudi, and it was then that she told me of her first suicide attempt. I was quite concerned, and fearing that she might try something rash again, I thought it would be better if Trudi did not have the pistol I had given her. When Trudi fell asleep, I quickly went home and retrieved the pistol from where she kept it.

When I got back to the hospital, Trudi was still asleep, and I saw her medical chart sitting next to her bed. I didn't really mean to look at it since those things are private, but I was so worried about her and I thought it might say something about how she was doing. It said that she had been sexually *Evidence Rule* assaulted when she was just out of high school and had had an abortion as a result. I couldn't believe Trudi had never told me about that. Hearing about that and her first suicide attempt made me realize how truly difficult her life had been. I decided that she needed me to help her get through it. Trudi needed to go with me to California.

When Trudi woke up in the morning, I suggested that we both leave for California to start a new life together. Trudi promised to think it over, but didn't commit herself to going.

Trudi was released that afternoon, and I drove her home. In order to frighten Trudi and help her realize how serious and stupid she was being with her life, I pointed to the pistol, which I knew was unloaded. I told Trudi how strong she was. How she had survived so much: two suicide attempts, the sexual assault, the abortion. I told Trudi that she was strong enough to not only live, but to learn to love life again. I told her that life, our life together, was worth living.

Then, to shock Trudi back into reality, I told Trudi, "If anybody's going to kill you, it will be me." She didn't say a word. She just stared back at me. I didn't recognize the look in her eyes, but it definitely wasn't fear. I don't know what it was.

When I went to work that night, November 27, I took the pistol that I had given to Trudi with me and put it in my locker at the police station. I was working the night shift, 9:00 p.m. to 5:30 a.m., and Sergeant Madden and I were on patrol together. I remember relating Trudi's suicide attempts and the incident with the gun to Madden, my immediate supervisor, later that night. I also told Madden of my plans to move to California and marry Trudi, but that I'd leave Nita City without her if she decided not to come with me. After work that night, the morning of November 28, I submitted my resignation to become effective December 1, three days later.

On the morning of December 1, I finished my shift at 5:30 a.m. as usual and packed my personal belongings into a suitcase. I cleaned out my locker and left my police equipment in the locker. My off-duty pistol was in the locker, and I put it into my shoulder harness. I didn't think about it at the time as I had the habit of carrying it while off duty. I had packed my car the day before, ready to move to California. I had picked up my stuff and Trudi's. I left my forwarding address (that of an old Marine buddy) at the police department, so my paycheck could be forwarded. I saw Sergeant Benbrook briefly on my way out, and Benbrook wished me luck. I left the police station and went to the Truck Stop Café to meet Trudi, who was scheduled to finish her shift at 6:00 a.m.

When I arrived at the truck stop, I saw Trudi sitting with some of the other servers in a booth. I wanted to talk to Trudi when she was alone, so I quietly went and sat in a booth at the other end where I could see her, but she couldn't see me without turning around. At 6:30, she got up and headed for the front door. I was worried she was going to leave without my getting a chance to talk to her, so I got up and chased after her. When I got to the front door, she was in the entrance entranceway, not about to leave, but merely using the vending machine there. This entranceway was between the door to the street and another door leading into the restaurant area itself. This latter door was glass and shut behind me, so I doubt anyone could hear what was being said. Also, my back was to it so anyone looking in would have a hard time seeing what was happening.

I told her I was about to leave for California and asked her if she would come with me. She said, "no." Then, she reached for the pistol in my holster. I suddenly remembered that I hadn't taken the bullets out like I usually do when I'm around her, and I was worried that she might think it wasn't loaded. I had made sure the safety was on before I put it in my holster that morning. She grabbed the pistol and released the safety. Fearing that she was about to harm herself, I tried to knock the gun out of her hand by hitting her arm from underneath. The gun jumped out of her hand and as we grabbed for it, my finger or Trudi's must have brushed the trigger, because it went off. I could see that Trudi was struck in the chest, she screamed. All the muscles in my body tensed. I screamed. The gun went off again.

Trudi fell to the ground, and I knelt beside her, holding her hand. She mumbled something inaudible; I told her that I loved her and I was sorry. The next thing I knew, the police arrived, and I went with them without resistance. I didn't talk to the police at first, because I was too stunned and shocked at what had happened. Later I got a lawyer, and he told me not to say anything to the police at all.

The pistol was already cocked when Trudi grabbed it. That morning I was carrying it with the hammer cocked and the safety on. I always carried it that way. Most of the other officers did as well. It's safe as long as the safety is on. When Trudi grabbed it, she flipped the safety off, just like I had taught her. That's when I got worried. I didn't know if she was just horsing around or if she really wanted to hurt herself. I can't imagine she was trying to hurt me. I just can't. I was worried about her, so I tried to get the gun away. I had to. She didn't know it was loaded.

I can't believe what happened. If only I would have knocked the gun down so it would have been on the floor. This has been a terrible and traumatic experience for me, and I can't talk about it anymore right now.

I hereby certify that this is a true and correct transcription of the statement made by John Diamond on December 1, YR-1, at the Nita City Police Station.

Certified by

Megan Schmidt

Megan Schmidt
Certified Shorthand Reporter (CSR)

OFFICE OF THE CORONER
DARROW COUNTY
NITA CITY, NITA 99995

December 3, YR-1

Sgt. E. A. Benbrook
Homicide Division
Nita City Police Department
Nita City, Nita

RE: Deceased Trudi Doyle
DOD: 12-1-YR-1

Dear Sgt. Benbrook:

Enclosed is a copy of the autopsy report for Ms. Trudi Doyle. There were five entry and exit bullet wounds: entry and exit wound on the right wrist; two entry wounds and one exit wound on the upper torso. The paths of the bullets in the upper torso were on a downward angle. A diagram reconstructing the entry, exit, and path of the bullets is appended to the autopsy report.

One bullet was recovered. It was placed in an evidence container that was sealed and marked with my initials. It will be sent to you by messenger, unless I receive other instructions.

Generally, my medical background is medical school, general internship, and residency in pathology at the Nita Medical Center. I am a board-certified pathologist, and my practice is limited to pathology. I completed my residency in YR-7, and I have been board certified since YR-5. I am presently a Deputy Coroner, and I have been with the office since YR-7.

If either your office or the prosecuting attorney desires further information in this regard, please contact me.

Sincerely,

Jamie Pierce
Jamie Pierce, MD
Deputy Coroner

JP:ns
Enclosure

Department of the Medical Examiner
Nita City

HC 8205

Case Title_____In Re Diamond, Nita City Police Department_____

Pathologist___Jamie Pierce, MD_____Autopsy No.__6172_____

Physician_____Darrow County Coroner, Nita City, Nita____Hospital No. NA_____

Patient Trudi Doyle__ Age 27_____Sex F_____ Race__W_____

Date, Hour–Death 12/1/YR-1_____Autopsy 12/1/YR-1, 10 a.m._M.E. No. 1-2315_____

Mortuary_____Darrow County Morgue_____

Clinical Data

At 7:10 a.m. on December 1, YR-1, the Coroner's Office was informed of a shooting death and instructed to proceed to the Truck Stop Café in Nita City, Nita, to obtain the body for autopsy. A person identified as Trudi Doyle, female, was found in the entranceway of the Truck Stop Café. Doyle was dead, and the body was transferred to the county morgue at approximately 7:30 a.m. by Coroner's Office personnel.

I began the postmortem examination at 10:00 a.m. Lateral and AP x-rays of the chest were taken prior to the autopsy; labeled with the date, autopsy number, and the letters "TD"; and then preserved. These were interpreted to show a solitary radiodense foreign body in the region of the right paraspinous musculature. Significant cardiomegaly was also noted.

Officer Smith (Nita City Police Department) was present during the postmortem examination. Postmortem photographs were taken by Officer Smith and Dr. Pierce.

Diagnoses

1. Gunshot wound to the right wrist.
2. Gunshot wound to the right anterior thorax.
3. Gunshot wound to the left anterior thorax.

Cause of Death

Massive right hemothorax secondary to gunshot wounds of the chest.

Postmortem Examination

General External Appearance

The body is that of a young adult Caucasian woman who measures sixty-four inches in length, weighs 130 pounds, and appears to be approximately the stated age. Postmortem rigidity is present in the muscles of mastication at the time of autopsy. Postmortem lividity is present posteriorly and is not fixed.

The arm span (reach) is 65½ inches.

General external appearance of the anterior and posterior thorax, anterior abdominal wall and flanks is normal.

General external appearance of the extremities is normal.

Clothing

The body was dressed in the following articles of clothing that were removed without alteration and labeled with the autopsy number, date, and letters TD: tan outer coat, white apron, yellow shirt, tan slacks, white cotton panties, white cotton brassiere, white socks, and black shoes, flat-heeled.

The tan outer coat is soaked with liquid and dried blood, and on each side of the midline of the frontal portion there is an approximately circular 8 mm in diameter hole. The fabric at the margins of these holes is frayed, but not charred, and powder residue cannot be found at the periphery of these holes with the unaided eye.

A battery watch with a damaged metal wrist band is worn on the decedent's right wrist. The watch has the correct time and is running.

External Injury

There is an approximately rectangular 1 by 0.8 cm wound on the external surface of the right wrist, centered at a point 1 cm medial and 1 cm proximal to the ulnar head. There is no evidence of powder deposition, stippling, or burning at the margins of this wound, but fragments of metal, similar in color and consistency, were found along the subcutaneous tract. This wound is consistent with a gunshot wound of entrance with an overlying intermediary target and is designated for purposes of reference as wound #1.

There is a "punched-out," irregularly margined, approximately circular 9 mm in diameter wound on the volar surface of the right wrist. There is a 2 mm abrasion collar at the margins of this wound, and no evidence of powder stippling, burning, or soot at the periphery of the wound. This wound is consistent with a shored wound of exit, and is designated as wound #2. The metal wrist band worn by the decedent does not overlie the volar tract of this wound.

There is an approximately 8 mm in diameter wound in the skin of the right anterior thorax, centered at a point 15 cm cephalad to the manubrial notch and 4.5 cm right lateral to the midline. A concentric 4 mm wide abrasion ring is at the periphery of this wound, and a 1 by 1 mm metallic foreign body, similar in color and consistency to that of the metal wrist band worn by the decedent, is embedded in the skin of the abrasion collar. There is no evidence of soot deposition, stippling, or burning at the margins or subcutaneous depths of this wound, which for purposes of reference is arbitrarily designated as wound #3.

There is an approximately circular 8 mm in diameter wound in the skin of the left anterior thorax, centered at a point 15 cm cephalad to the manubrial notch and 5 cm left lateral to the midline. A 2 mm wide abrasion collar is at the margin of this wound, and there is no evidence of burning, stippling, or soot deposition at the periphery or subcutaneous depths of the wound. For purposes of reference, this wound is arbitrarily designated as wound #4.

There is a 1 cm laceration in the skin of the right posterior thorax, centered at a point 20 cm caudad to the lowest crease of the neck and 3 cm right lateral to the midline. There is no evidence of marginal abrasion at the periphery of this wound. This wound is consistent with a gunshot wound of exit and this wound is arbitrarily designated as wound #5.

There are no other external injuries.

Internal Examination

The subcutaneous fat of the abdomen is 1 to 1.5 cm thick, and the subcutaneous fat of the thorax is approximately 1 cm thick. Each of the abdominal organs is present and is located in its normal anatomical situs. The peritoneal surfaces are smooth and glistening. The left subdiaphragmatic space contains approximately 15 cc of clotted and nonclotted blood.

The right chest cavity contains approximately 2000 cc of clotted and nonclotted blood. The left chest cavity contains approximately 25 cc of straw-colored serous fluid.

Internal Injury

A tract is followed from the wound on the extensor surface of the right wrist through the subcutaneous fat, interosseous ligament, and tendon of the palmaris longus muscle. It exits through the wound on the volar surface of the wrist. Major arteries, veins, and nerves are not involved within the tract of this wound.

A tract, which for purposes of reference is arbitrarily designated as tract A, is followed from wound #3 in the right anterior thorax through the space between the fifth and sixth costal cartilage, into the pericardial sac and through the epicardium, myocardium, and endocardium of the anterior then posterior walls of the right ventricle, exiting the posterior portion of the pericardial sac into a laceration of the right branch of the pulmonary artery and right mainstem bronchus, through the parenchyma of the right middle lobe and into the space between the third and fourth ribs posteriorly, and into the right paraspinous musculature. A severely distorted metal projectile is removed from the terminal point of this tract and is placed in a labeled bullet envelope.

There is approximately 2000 cc of clotted and nonclotted blood within the right chest cavity, as described above, and in addition there is hemorrhage along the tract of this wound from the point of entrance in the right anterior thorax to the point of termination in the right paraspinous musculature. Approximately 500 cc of blood was found in the pericardial sac, which is a finding in cardiac tamponade.

The trajectory of this tract (A) makes an angle of approximately 5 degrees to a sagittal plane and 15 degrees caudad to a transverse plane, which is slightly downward when measured from the front to the back of the decedent.

A tract, which for purposes of reference is arbitrarily designated as tract B, is followed from wound #4 in the left anterior thorax through the left anterior thorax through the costal cartilage of the sixth and seventh ribs, though the dome of the left hemidiaphragm and into the inferiormost portion of the pericardial sac without involvement of the heart itself, across the midline and into the dome of the right hemidiaphragm, into the inferiormost portion of the right of the right chest cavity and a 1 by 6 cm laceration of the anterobasal segment of the right upper lung lobe, into a 1 cm wound of the posterior parietal pleura between the fifth and sixth ribs, into the right paraspinous musculature and through the exit wound #5 in the right posterior thorax.

The trajectory of this tract (B) makes an angle of approximately 30 degrees medial to a sagittal plane and 10 degrees caudad to a transverse plane, which is downward and from the left to right when measured from the front to the back to the decedent.

There are no other internal injuries.

Respiratory System

The right lung has a mass of 250 grams and is collapsed. The left lung has a mass of 325 grams and is fully expanded. The pulmonary artery segments are normal, except as described above. The segmental and subsegmental bronchi contain approximately 15 to 20 cc of liquid and dried blood, but are otherwise normal. The parenchyma of the left lung is normal. The cut surfaces of the right lung are normal except for atelectasis.

Cardiovascular System

The heart has a mass of 280 grams. The cardiac valves are thin and pliable, and the coronary arteries are free of atheromatous plaque formation.

The tunneling tract of the projectile through the anterior and posterior walls of the right ventricle created a cardiac tamponade where the normally potential space between the pericardium and heart muscle is filled with blood. The right ventricular wall is 3 mm thick, and the left ventricular wall is 11 mm thick. The myocardium has a uniform red-brown color and is normal.

The thoracic and abdominal portions of the aorta are normal.

Hepatobiliary System

The gall bladder wall is thin and pliable and the lumen contains approximately 25 cc of green-black bile and no stones. The parenchyma is firm and has areas of nodularity. Notably, the liver tissue is not uniformly brown in color and has areas of scarring.

The liver has a mass of 1260 grams; the capsule of the liver is intact, except for the diaphragmatic reflection of the right lobe. The parenchyma is firm and has a uniform tan-brown color.

Lymphoid System

Para-aortic, hilar, and para-tracheal lymph nodes are small and appear normal.

The spleen has a mass of 110 grams. The capsule is intact, and the red pulp is firm. Lymphoid tissue is easily discernible and is represented by uniform 0.5 mm in diameter aggregates of gray-white tissue scattered throughout the parenchyma.

Pancreas and Adrenals

The pancreas and adrenals are normal.

Genitourinary System

Each kidney has a mass of 120 grams. The capsules of the kidneys are intact and the corticomedullary injunctions are distinct. The pelves and ureters are normal.

The bladder contains approximately 150 cc of clear yellow urine. The bladder mucosa is normal.

Gastrointestinal System

The esophageal and gastric mucosa are intact. The stomach contains approximately 300 cc of incompletely digested particulate food matter.

The small intestine, appendix, and large bowel are normal.

Brain and Central Nervous System

The calvarium is of average thickness, and there is no evidence of subgaleal, subdural, or subarachnoid hemorrhage.

The brain has a mass of 1280 grams. The gyri of the cerebral hemispheres are normally prominent, and the sulci are normally narrow. Serial coronal sections of the cerebrum and serial transverse sections of the cerebrum and serial transverse sections of the cerebellum are normal. The midbrain, pons, and medulla are normal.

Neck Structures

The hyoid bone and thyroid cartilage are intact.

The lobes of the thyroid gland have approximately equal mass and have a uniform bright red-brown color and a normal firm texture. Parathyroid tissue is difficult to isolate, and none is found.

The cervical portion of the esophageal mucosa is normal.

The larynx and main stem bronchi contain aspirated blood, as described above.

Toxicology

For purposes of a blood alcohol determination, blood is aspirated from the left atrium of the heart during performance of the postmortem examination. An aliquot of urine, a portion of liver, and the gastric contests are also saved.

Comment

Microscopic examination will not be performed at this time. However, representative portions of each organ will be embedded in paraffin and will be available for microscopic examination if it becomes necessary at a future date.

Addendum

The postmortem blood alcohol level is 0.008 g/dL. Postmortem vitreous chemistries are within normal limits.

Jamie Pierce

Jamie Pierce, MD
Deputy Coroner
Darrow County
Nita City, Nita 99995

Dictated 12-1-YR-1 Signed 12-3-YR-1

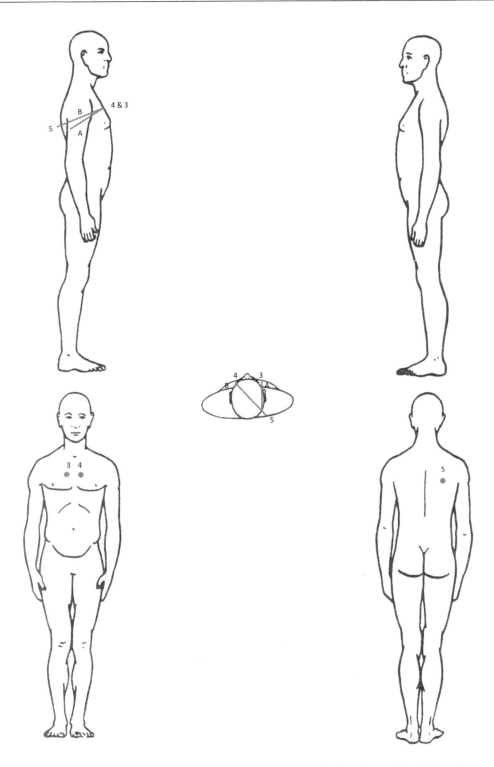

Diagram reconstructing entry, exit, and path of bullets through decedent, Trudi Doyle.

Jamie Pierce

Jamie Pierce, MD
Deputy Coroner

Memorial Hospital Report: Emergency Room Treatment No. 04535	Name	First Trudi		Middle Ann		Last Doyle		
	Sex F	Age 27	Date of Admission 11/26/YR-1	Time of Admission 3:20 p.m.	Date of Discharge 11/27/YR-1	Time of Discharge 3:00 p.m.		
	Address Street 1243 Maple Lane			City Nita City			State NI	Zip 99995
	Telephone Number (828) 555-0979		Brought in by P.O. John Diamond		Relationship			
Insurance Provider Blue Cross			Policy Number 663392559			Group Number 001-555-972		
Employer Truck Stop Cafe	Employer Phone (828) 555-3266		Employer Address Street Highway 33		City Nita City		State NI	Zip 99995
Vital Signs B.P. 100/55 P. 43 T. 98.6 R. 12	Examining Physician K. Troyer, MD		Family Doctor W. Raycoff, MD			Nurse's Initials S.J.		
	☐ X-Ray	☐ EKG		☐ Lab		☐ Pharm	☐ M & S	

Allergies

History

Patient swallowed bottle of Nembutal. Unknown no. of pills.
Had been very depressed the last week.
Prior surgeries: abortion, YR-9, after sexual assault.

Exam

Patient semi-comatose. Responds poorly to pain stimulae. Voice, speech slurred. Respiration slow and shallow. Pulse poor quality. Temp. normal. No outward sign of head injury. Pupils round, regular, equal.

Treatment

Stomach pumped. Blood barbit. level drawn.

Diagnosis

Barbituate poisoning.

Disposition of Patient Held	Referred to:	DL	Hospital X	Home	Other:	Condition of Patient on Discharge recovered

Certified as a true and correct copy of the original in the medical files of Memorial Hospital.

William Coleman

William Coleman
Medical Record Librarian

Diagram of Beretta 84FS Cheetah Semi-Automatic
(hand drawn by Sgt. Benbrook)

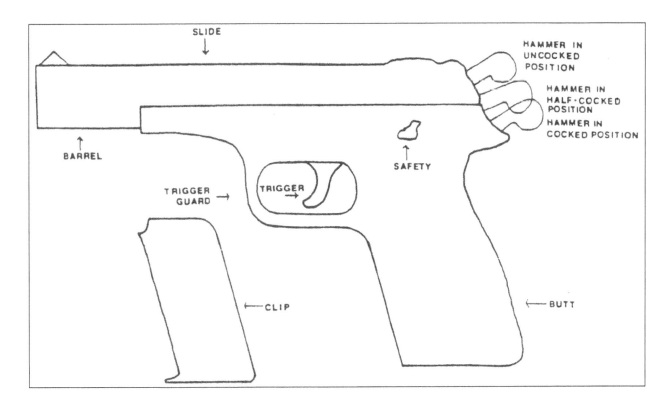

Beretta 84FS Cheetah (Labeled)

1) Barrel
2) Open slide design
3) Firing pin block (prevents pistol from firing if dropped)
4) Sights
5) Ambidextrous safety (accommodates right- and left-handed shooters)
6) Reversible magazine release (accommodates right- and left-handed shooters)
7) Anodized alloy frame
8) Trigger guard
9) Double-action trigger

Thirteen- or ten-round magazines

Operation of Beretta 84FS Cheetah Semi-Automatic

1. Bullets are placed in the magazine. This model's magazine holds thirteen rounds.

2. The magazine is inserted in the end of the butt of the gun.

3. A bullet is inserted into the firing chamber. This procedure, called chambering a round, is performed by pulling back and releasing the slide. This also cocks the hammer, thus readying the gun to fire.

4. When a round is chambered and the hammer cocked, the gun may be placed in an uncocked position by manipulating the safety/de-cocker lever.

5. When the magazine is loaded and the pistol is fired, the gas behind the exiting bullet forces the slide mechanism back, thus automatically ejecting the spent shell, forcing the hammer back into the cocked position and, while sliding forward again, chambering a new bullet. The pistol is then ready to be fired again by merely pulling the trigger.

6. Because this gun will not be actually loaded or fired in courtroom demonstrations, the chambering of the each round between pulling the trigger must be performed manually, as described in paragraph 3.

7. The safety is a small catch that when released will prevent the gun from firing even though it is cocked. It must be released manually.

8. The pistol may also fire with the hammer down, in double-action mode (like a revolver). The trigger pull is substantially heavier in the double-action mode.

Beretta Cheetah 84FS Specifications

Caliber: .380 caliber

Action: Double or Single Action

Overall Length: 6.77 inches

Height: 4.8 inches

Width over grips: 1.37 inches

Length of barrel: 3.81 inches

Distance between front and rear sights: 4.88 inches

Unloaded weight: 23.3 oz.

Magazine capacity: 13 rounds

Bullet size: 90 grains (jacketed hollow point)

Muzzle velocity: 1000 ft/s

Energy: 200 ft/lbf

Applicable Nita Statutes

Nita Criminal Code, Chapter 40.

Section 18-3-101. Homicide, definition of terms.

1. Homicide means the killing of a person by another.

2. Person, when referring to the victim of a homicide, means a human being who had been born and was alive at the time of the homicidal act.

3. The term after deliberation means not only intentionally, but also that the decision to commit the act has been made after the exercise of reflection and judgment concerning the act. An act committed after deliberation is never one that has been committed in a hasty or impulsive manner.

Section 18-3-102. Murder in the first degree.

1. A person commits the crime of murder in the first degree if:

    a. After deliberation and with the intent to cause the death of a person other than himself, he causes the death of that person or of another person.

2. Murder in the first degree is a class 1 felony.

Section 18-3-103. Murder in the second degree.

1. A person commits the crime of murder in the second degree if:

    a. She intentionally, but not after deliberation, causes the death of a person; or

    b. With intent to cause serious bodily injury to a person other than herself, she causes the death of that person or of another person.

2. Diminished responsibility due to lack of mental capacity is not a defense to murder in the second degree.

3. Murder in the second degree is a class 2 felony.

Section 18-3-104. Manslaughter.

1. A person commits the crime of manslaughter if:

    a. He recklessly causes the death of a person; or

    b. He intentionally, but not after deliberation, causes the death of a person, under circumstances where the act causing the death was performed upon a sudden heat of passion caused by a serious and highly provoking act of the intended victim, affecting the person killing sufficiently to excite an irresistible passion in a reasonable person; but if between the provocation and the killing there is an interval sufficient for the voice of reason and humanity to be heard, the killing is murder.

2. Manslaughter is a class 4 felony.

Section 18-3-105. Criminally negligent homicide.

1. A person commits the crime of criminally negligent homicide if:

    a. By conduct amounting to criminal negligence, she causes the death of a person; or

    b. She intentionally causes the death of a person, but she believes in good faith that circumstances exist that would justify the act under §§ 18-1-701 and 18-1-702, but her belief that such circumstances exist is unreasonable.

2. Criminally negligent homicide is a class 1 misdemeanor.

Section 18-1-105. Felonies classified, penalties.

Felonies are divided into four classes that are distinguished from one another by the following penalties that are authorized upon conviction:

Class	Minimum Sentence	Maximum Sentence
1	50 years imprisonment	Life imprisonment
2	10 years imprisonment	50 years imprisonment
3	5 years imprisonment	40 years imprisonment
4	1 year imprisonment, or two thousand dollars fine	10 years imprisonment, or thirty thousand dollars fine, or

Section 18-1-106. Misdemeanors classified, penalties.

Misdemeanors are divided into three classes that are distinguished from one another by the following penalties that are authorized upon conviction:

Class	Minimum Sentence	Maximum Sentence
1	12 months imprisonment, or one thousand dollars fine, or both	24 months imprisonment, or five thousand dollars fine, or both
2	6 months imprisonment, or five hundred dollars fine, or both	12 months imprisonment, or one thousand dollars fine, or both
3	Fifty dollars fine	6 months imprisonment, or five hundred dollars fine, or both

No term of imprisonment for conviction of a misdemeanor shall be served in the state penitentiary unless served concurrently with a term for conviction of a felony.

Section 18-1-501. Principles of criminal culpability, definitions.

The following definitions are applicable to the determination of culpability requirements for offenses defined in this code:

1. Act means a bodily movement and includes words and possession of property.

2. Conduct means an act or omission and its accompanying state of mind or, where relevant, a series of acts or omissions.

3. Criminal negligence. A person acts with criminal negligence when, through a gross deviation from the standard of care that a reasonable person would exercise, he fails to perceive a substantial and unjustifiable risk that a result will occur or that a circumstance exists.

4. Culpable mental state means intentionally, or knowingly, or recklessly, or with criminal negligence as these terms are defined in this section.

5. Intentionally. A person acts intentionally with respect to a result or to a conduct described by a statute defining an offense when his conscious objective is to cause such result or to engage in such conduct.

6. Knowingly. A person acts knowingly with respect to conduct or to a circumstance described by a statute defining an offense when she is aware that her conduct is of such nature or that such circumstance exists.

7. Omission means a failure to perform an act to which a duty or performance is imposed by law.

8. Recklessly. A person acts recklessly when he consciously disregards a substantial and unjustifiable risk that a result will occur or that a circumstance exists.

9. Voluntary act means an act performed consciously as a result of effort or determination and includes the possession of property if the actor was aware of her physical possession or control thereof for a sufficient period to have been able to terminate it.

Sections 18-1-701 and 18-1-702. Justification and Exemption from Criminal Responsibility.

Section 18-1-701. Use of physical force, special relationship.

The use of physical force upon another person that would otherwise constitute an offense is justifiable and not criminal under any of the following circumstances:

* * *

3. A person acting under a reasonable belief that another person is about to commit suicide or to inflict serious physical injury upon himself may use reasonable and appropriate physical force upon that person to the extent that it is reasonably necessary to thwart the result.

Section 18-1-702. Use of physical force in defense of a person.

1. A person is justified in using physical force upon another person in order to defend herself or a third person from what she reasonably believes to be the use or imminent use of unlawful physical force by that other person, and she may use a degree of force that she reasonably believes to be necessary for that purpose.

2. Deadly physical force may be used only if a person reasonably believes a lesser degree of force is inadequate, and the actor has reasonable ground to believe, and does believe, that he or another person is in imminent danger of being killed or receiving great bodily harm.

3. Notwithstanding the provisions of subsection (1), a person is not justified in using physical force if:

   a. With intent to cause physical injury or death to another person, she provokes the use of unlawful physical force by that other person; or

b. She is the initial aggressor; or

c. The physical force involved is the product of a combat by agreement not specifically authorized by law.

Justification and Affirmative Defenses, Nita Supreme Court

State v. Pierizak, 78 Nita 2d 68 (YR-4). The criminal case law in Nita is well settled that for affirmative defenses involving principles of justification, the burden of proof is on the State. The defendant has the burden of going forward by raising the defense and presenting some evidence of the defense. But once that is done, the burden of proof is on the State to prove each element of the crime charged, including the issue raised by the defense of justification. The term "affirmative defense" is somewhat misleading because the burden is not on the defendant to prove the defense. Under § 18-1-606 of the Nita Criminal Code, once the issue of the defense is raised by "some evidence," the State "must sustain the burden of proving the defendant guilty beyond a reasonable doubt as to that issue together with all the other elements of the offense." *See also State v. Meninger,* 198 Nita 351 (YR-22).

Proposed Jury Instructions

The following jury instructions are intended for use with any of the files contained in these materials regardless of whether the trial is in Nita state court or in federal court. In addition, each of these files contains special instructions dealing with the law applicable in the particular case. The instructions set forth here state general principles that may be applicable in any of the cases and may be used at the discretion of the trial judge.*

Part I: Preliminary Instructions

(Given prior to the evidence.)

Nita Instruction 01:01. Introduction

You have been selected as jurors and have taken an oath to well and truly try this case. This trial will last one day.

During the progress of the trial there will be periods of time when the Court recesses. During those periods of time, you must not talk about this case among yourselves or with anyone else.

During the trial, do not talk to any of the parties, their lawyers, or any of the witnesses.

If any attempt is made by anyone to talk to you concerning the matters here under consideration, you should immediately report that fact to the Court.

You should keep an open mind. You should not form or express an opinion during the trial and should reach no conclusion in this case until you have heard all of the evidence, the arguments of counsel, and the final instructions as to the law that will be given to you by the Court.

Nita Instruction 01:02. Conduct of the Trial

First, the attorneys will have an opportunity to make opening statements. These statements are not evidence and should be considered only as a preview of what the attorneys expect the evidence will be.

Following the opening statements, witnesses will be called to testify. They will be placed under oath and questioned by the attorneys. Documents and other tangible exhibits may also be received as evidence. If an exhibit is given to you to examine, you should examine it carefully, individually, and without comment.

It is counsel's right and duty to object when testimony or other evidence is being offered that he believes is not admissible.

When the Court sustains an objection to a question, the jurors must disregard the question and the answer, if one has been given, and draw no inference from the question or answer or speculate as to what the witness would have said if permitted to answer. Jurors must also disregard evidence stricken from the record.

When the Court sustains an objection to any evidence, the jurors must disregard the evidence.

---

* The instructions contained in this section are borrowed or adapted from a number of sources, including California, Illinois, Indiana, Washington, and Colorado pattern jury instructions.

When the Court overrules an objection to any evidence, the jurors must not give that evidence any more weight than if the objection had not been made.

When the evidence is completed, the attorneys will make final statements. These final statements are not evidence, but are given to assist you in evaluating the evidence. The attorneys are also permitted to argue in an attempt to persuade you to a particular verdict. You may accept or reject those arguments as you see fit.

Finally, just before you retire to consider your verdict, I will give you further instructions on the law that applies to this case.

Part II: Final Instructions

(Given after the parties have rested.)

General Principles

Nita Instruction 2:01. Introduction

Members of the jury, the evidence and arguments in this case have been completed, and I will now instruct you as to the law.

The law applicable to this case is stated in these instructions, and it is your duty to follow all of the instructions. You must not single out certain instructions and disregard others.

It is your duty to determine the facts and to determine them only from the evidence in this case. You are to apply the law to the facts and in this way decide the case. You must not be governed or influenced by sympathy or prejudice for or against any party in this case. Your verdict must be based on evidence and not on speculation, guess, or conjecture.

From time to time the court has ruled on the admissibility of evidence. You must not concern yourselves with the reasons for these rulings. You should disregard questions and exhibits that were withdrawn or on which objections were sustained.

You should also disregard testimony and exhibits that the court has refused or stricken.

The evidence that you should consider consists only of the witnesses' testimonies and the exhibits the court has received.

Any evidence that was received for a limited purpose should not be considered by you for any other purpose.

You should consider all the evidence in the light of your own observations and experiences in life.

Neither by these instructions nor by any ruling or remark that I have made do I mean to indicate any opinion as to the facts or as to what your verdict should be.

Nita Instruction 2:02. Opening Statements and Closing Arguments

Opening statements are made by the attorneys to acquaint you with the facts they expect to prove. Closing arguments are made by the attorneys to discuss the facts and circumstances in the case and should be confined to the evidence and to reasonable inferences to be drawn therefrom. Neither opening statements nor closing arguments are evidence, and any statement or argument made by the attorneys that is not based on the evidence should be disregarded.

Nita Instruction 2:03. Credibility of Witnesses

You are the sole judges of the credibility of the witnesses and of the weight to be given to the testimony of each witness. In determining what credit is to be given any witness, you may take into account the witness's ability and opportunity to observe; the witness's manner and appearance while testifying; any interest, bias, or prejudice the witness may have; the reasonableness of the witness's testimony considered in light of all the evidence; and any other factors that bear on the believability and weight of the witness's testimony.

Nita Instruction 2:04. Expert Witnesses

You have heard evidence in this case from witnesses who testified as experts. The law allows experts to express an opinion on subjects involving their special knowledge, training and skill, experience, or research. While their opinions are allowed to be given, it is entirely within the province of the jury to determine what weight shall be given their testimony. Jurors are not bound by the testimony of experts; their testimony is to be weighed as that of any other witness.

Nita Instruction 2:05. Direct and Circumstantial Evidence

The law recognizes two kinds of evidence: direct and circumstantial. Direct evidence proves a fact directly; that is, the evidence by itself, if true, establishes the fact. Circumstantial evidence is the proof of facts or circumstances that give rise to a reasonable inference of other facts; that is, circumstantial evidence process a fact indirectly in that it follows from other facts or circumstances according to common experience and observations in life. An eyewitness is a common example of direct evidence while human footprints are circumstantial evidence that a person was present.

The law makes no distinction between direct and circumstantial evidence as to the degree or amount of proof required, and each should be considered according to whatever weight or value it may have. All of the evidence should be considered and evaluated by you in arriving at your verdict.

Nita Instruction 2:06. Concluding Instruction

I did not in any way, and do not by these instructions, give or intimate any opinions as to what has or has not been proven in the case, or as to what are or are not the facts of the case.

No one of these instructions states all of the law applicable, but all of them must be taken, read, and considered together as they are connected with and related to each other as a whole.

You must not be concerned with the wisdom of any rule of law. Regardless of any opinions you may have as to what the law ought to be, it would be a violation of your sworn duty to base a verdict on any other view of the law than that given in these instructions.

Nita Instruction 3:01. Indictment (Information)

The indictment in this case is the formal method of accusing the defendant of a crime and placing him on trial. It is not any evidence against the defendant and does not create any inference of guilt. The State has the burden of proving beyond a reasonable doubt every essential element of the crime charged in the indictment or any of the crimes included therein.

Nita Instruction 3:02. Burden of Proof

The State has the burden of proving the guilt of the defendant beyond a reasonable doubt, and this burden remains on the State throughout the case. The defendant is not required to prove his innocence.

Nita Instruction 3:03. Reasonable Doubt

Reasonable doubt means a doubt based on reason and common sense that arises from a fair and rational consideration of all the evidence or lack of evidence in the case. It is a doubt that is not a vague, speculative, or imaginary doubt, but such a doubt as would cause reasonable persons to hesitate to act in matters of importance to themselves.

Nita Instruction 3:04. Presumption of Innocence

The defendant is presumed to be innocent of the charges against him. This presumption remains with him throughout every stage of the trial and during your deliberations on the verdict. The presumption is not overcome until, from all the evidence in the case, you are convinced beyond a reasonable doubt that the defendant is guilty.

Nita Instruction 3:05. Reputation/Character

The defendant has introduced evidence of his character and reputation for (truth and veracity) (being a peaceful and law-abiding citizen) (morality) (chastity) (honesty and integrity) (etc.). This evidence may be sufficient when considered with the other evidence in the case to raise a reasonable doubt of the defendant's guilt. However, if from all the evidence in the case you are satisfied beyond a reasonable doubt of the defendant's guilt, then it is your duty to find him guilty, even though he may have a good reputation for_____.

CASE-SPECIFIC INSTRUCTIONS

1. The court will now instruct you on the law governing this case. You must arrive at your verdict by unanimous vote, applying the law, as you are now instructed, to the facts as you find them to be.

2. The State of Nita has charged the defendant, John Diamond, with the crime of first-degree murder, which includes the crimes of second-degree murder, manslaughter, and criminally negligent homicide. The defendant has pleaded not guilty.

3. Under the criminal code of the State of Nita, a person commits the crime of first-degree murder if, after deliberation and with the intent to cause the death of a person other than himself, he causes the death of that person or of another person.

    Person, when referring to the victim of a homicide, means a human being who had been born and was alive at the time of the homicidal act.

    After deliberation means not only intentionally, but also that the decision to commit the act has been made after the exercise of reflection and judgment concerning the act. An act committed after deliberation is never one that has been committed in a hasty or impulsive manner.

4. Under the criminal code of the State of Nita, a person commits the crime of second-degree murder if,

    a. He intentionally, but not after deliberation, causes the death of another person; or

    b. With intent to cause serious injury to a person other than himself, he causes the death of that person.

    Intentionally. A person acts intentionally with respect to a result or to conduct described by a statute defining a crime when his conscious objective is to cause such result or to engage in such conduct.

5. Under the criminal code of the State of Nita, a person commits the crime of manslaughter if,

    a. He recklessly causes the death of a person; or

    b. He intentionally, but not after deliberation, causes the death of a person, under circumstances where the act causing the death was performed upon a sudden heat of passion caused by a serious and highly provoking act of the intended victim, but if between the provocation and the killing there is an interval sufficient for the voice of reason and humanity to be heard, the killing is murder.

    Recklessly. A person acts recklessly when he consciously disregards a substantial and unjustifiable risk that a result will occur or that a circumstance exists.

6. Under the criminal code of the State of Nita, a person commits the crime of criminally negligent homicide if,

    a. By conduct amounting to criminal negligence he causes the death of a person; or

    b. He intentionally causes the death of a person, but he believes in good faith that circumstances exist that would justify his conduct, but his belief that such circumstances exist is unreasonable.

Conduct means an act or omission and its accompanying state of mind, or a series of acts or omissions.

Criminal negligence. A person acts with criminal negligence when, through a gross deviation from the standard of care that a reasonable person would exercise, he fails to perceive a substantial and unjustifiable risk that a result will occur or that a circumstance exists.

7. The use of physical force on another person is justifiable and not criminal when a person acts under a reasonable belief that another person is about to commit suicide or to inflict serious bodily injury upon herself and he uses reasonable and appropriate physical force upon that person to the extent that it is reasonably necessary to thwart the result.

8. A person is justified in using physical force upon another person in order to defend himself or a third person from what he reasonably believes to be the use or imminent use of unlawful physical force by that other person, and he may use a degree of force that he reasonably believes to be necessary for that purpose.

    However, deadly physical force upon another person may be used only if a person reasonably believes a lesser degree of force is inadequate and the actor has reasonable ground to believe, and does believe, that he or another person is in imminent danger of being killed or of receiving great bodily harm.

9. To sustain the charge of first-degree murder, the state must prove the following propositions:

    a. That the defendant performed the acts that caused the death of Trudi Doyle, a human being; and

    b. That defendant acted after deliberation and with the intent to cause the death of Trudi Doyle or any other person.

    If you find from your consideration of all the evidence that each of these propositions has been proved beyond a reasonable doubt, then you should find the defendant guilty of first-degree murder.

    If, on the other hand, you find from your consideration of all the evidence that either of these propositions has not been proved beyond a reasonable doubt, then you should find the defendant not guilty of first-degree murder.

10. To sustain the charge of second-degree murder, the State must prove the following propositions:

    a. That the defendant performed the acts that caused the death of Trudi Doyle, a human being; and

    b. The defendant intended to kill or cause serious bodily injury to Trudi Doyle; and

    c. That the defendant was not justified in using the force that he used.

    If you find from your consideration of all the evidence that each of these propositions has been proved beyond a reasonable doubt, then you should find the defendant guilty of second-degree murder.

    If, on the other hand, you find from your consideration of all the evidence that any of these propositions has not been proved beyond a reasonable doubt, then you should find the defendant not guilty of second-degree murder.

11. To sustain the charge of manslaughter, the State must prove the following propositions:

    a. That the defendant performed the acts that caused the death of Trudi Doyle, a human being; and

    b. That the defendant acted recklessly; or he acted intentionally, but under a sudden heat of passion caused by a serious and highly provoking action by Trudi Doyle.

    If you find from your consideration of all the evidence that each of these propositions has been proved beyond a reasonable doubt, then you should find the defendant guilty of manslaughter.

    If, on the other hand, you find from your consideration of all the evidence that either of these propositions has not been proved beyond a reasonable doubt, then you should find the defendant not guilty of manslaughter.

12. To sustain the charge of criminally negligent homicide, the State must prove the following propositions:

    a. That the defendant performed the acts that caused the death of Trudi Doyle, a human being; and

    b. That the defendant acted with criminal negligence; or he acted intentionally, but believed in good faith that circumstances existed that would have justified the killing of Trudi Doyle, and the defendant's belief that such circumstances existed was unreasonable.

    If you find from your consideration of all the evidence that each of these propositions has been proved beyond a reasonable doubt, then you should find the defendant guilty of criminally negligent homicide.

    If, on the other hand, you find from your consideration of all the evidence that either of these propositions has not been proved beyond a reasonable doubt, then you should find the defendant not guilty of criminally negligent homicide.

13. The unintentional killing of a human being is excusable and not unlawful when committed by accident in the performance of a lawful act by lawful means and where the person causing the death acted with that care and caution that would be exercised by an ordinarily careful and prudent individual under like circumstances.

    If you find that Trudi Doyle lost her life by such an accident, then you should find the defendant not guilty.

14. When a person commits an act by accident under circumstances that show no evil design, intention, or culpable negligence, he does not thereby commit a crime.

    If you find that Trudi Doyle lost her life by such an accident, then you should find the defendant not guilty.

IN THE CIRCUIT COURT OF
DARROW COUNTY, NITA

THE PEOPLE OF THE STATE OF NITA	)	
	)	
v.	)	Case No. CR2216
	)	
JOHN DIAMOND,	)	JURY VERDICT
Defendant.	)	

We, the Jury, return the following verdict, and each of us concurs in this verdict: [Choose the appropriate verdict]

NOT GUILTY

We, the Jury, find the defendant, John Diamond, NOT GUILTY.

_____

Foreperson

OR
FIRST-DEGREE MURDER

We, the Jury, find the defendant, John Diamond, GUILTY of Murder in the First Degree.

_____

Foreperson

OR
SECOND-DEGREE MURDER

We, the Jury, find the defendant, John Diamond, GUILTY of Murder in the Second Degree.

_____

Foreperson

OR
MANSLAUGHTER

We, the Jury, find the defendant, John Diamond, GUILTY of Manslaughter.

_____

Foreperson

OR
CRIMINALLY NEGLIGENT HOMICIDE

We, the Jury, find the defendant, John Diamond, GUILTY of Criminally Negligent Homicide.

_____

Foreperson

STATE V. DOYLE

CONTENTS

INTRODUCTION TO STATE V. DOYLE

A grand jury has charged Trudi Doyle with first-degree murder in the December 1, YR-1, shooting death of Johnny Diamond at the Truck Stop Café on Highway 33 outside of Nita City.

Truck Stop Café is on the outskirts of Nita City—bridging a housing development and farms, mostly small vegetable and fruit farms, and a few nurseries. A greenbelt area with some dairy and grain farms are between the Truck Stop Café, small farms, and the next town.

Ms. Doyle and Mr. Diamond had been living together for two months immediately prior to her death. Ms. Doyle was a server at the Truck Stop Café, and Mr. Diamond was a police officer with the Nita City Police Department. Both Ms. Doyle and Mr. Diamond worked night shifts.

On the morning of December 1, YR-1, Mr. Diamond, who had just resigned from the Nita City Police Department, went to the Truck Stop Café to meet Ms. Doyle, who got off work at 6:00 a.m. He sat in a booth. Ms. Doyle was sitting in a booth at the other side of the restaurant talking with the other servers. She did not speak to Mr. Diamond, and then at 6:30 a.m., Ms. Doyle got up from the booth and went to the entranceway of the café. Mr. Diamond followed her, and they talked for a few minutes. Two shots rang out. Mr. Diamond slumped to the floor and died within minutes. Ms. Doyle remained at the scene and was arrested when the police arrived.

The applicable law is contained in the statutes and the proposed jury instructions set forth at the end of the file.

All years in these materials are stated in the following form:

YR-0   indicates the current, actual year in which the students are trying the case (e.g., please use "2016," not "YR-0" when presenting the case);

YR-1   indicates the previous year (e.g., 2015, if 2016 is the current year);

YR-2   indicates the second preceding year, etc. (e.g., 2014, if 2016 is the current year).

Instructions for Use as a Full Trial

When this case file is used for a full trial, the following witnesses are available. Diamond is male and Doyle is female; every other witness may be male or female. **Each witness' first name is determined by the gender of the person playing the witness role.**

State: E. A. Benbrook

Joseph/JoAnn Foster

Beth/Brian Kelly

Dr. Jamie Pierce

Defense: Trudy Dole, accused [must be called in a mock trial]

Eric/Estelle Mason

Jeanne/John Madden

Each party must call *two* witnesses to testify.

Each party may petition the court for the admission of facts from a witness not called. The moving party must show that the fact(s) would be admissible if the witness were called to testify and the need.

Required Stipulations

1. The facts in the Introduction are agreed facts and admissible without further proof.

2. Neutron activation tests of Trudi Doyle's hands were positive

3. Neutron activation tests of Johnny Diamond's hands were negative.

4. Test of powder burns on Johnny Diamond's jacket were inconclusive due to extensive bleeding.

5. Blood on the jacket was type O negative. Johnny Diamond has type O negative blood.

6. Comparison of the bullet found in Johnny Diamond's body with a bullet fired from Diamond's gun show that both were fired from that gun.

7. The gun was examined for fingerprints, but no usable prints were found.

8. The gun has a trigger pull of six pounds. This is an average pull, midway between a hair trigger and a heavy trigger pull.

9. When fired, the gun recoils approximately 15 degrees.

10. The Memorial Hospital medical records were made and kept in the regular course of the hospital's business. William Coleman, the medical records librarian, would so testify if called as a witness.

11. The transcript of the statement given by Trudi Doyle is authentic.

12. The Beretta 84FS Cheetah in the photograph is the pistol Sergeant Benbrook retrieved from the Truck Stop Café on December 1, YR-1.

13. Johnny Diamond has owned the pistol pictured in the photograph ever since he bought it while serving in the military.

IN THE CIRCUIT COURT OF
DARROW COUNTY, NITA

THE PEOPLE OF THE STATE OF NITA	)	
	)	
v.	)	Case No. CR2216
	)	
TRUDI DOYLE,	)	INDICTMENT
Defendant.	)	

The Grand Jury in and for the county of Darrow, State of Nita, upon their oath and in the name and by the authority of the State of Nita, does hereby charge the following offense under the Criminal Code of the State of Nita:

That on December 1, YR-1, at and within the County of Darrow in the State of Nita, Trudi Doyle committed the crime of

MURDER IN THE FIRST DEGREE

in violation of Section 18-3-102 of the Nita Criminal Code of 1974, as amended, in that she, after deliberation and with the intent to cause the death of a person other than herself, caused the death of Johnny Diamond with a deadly weapon, namely a Beretta semi-automatic pistol.

Contrary to the form of the Statute and against the peace and dignity of the People of the State of Nita.

A TRUE BILL:

Jeanne Mitchell

Jeanne Mitchell
Foreperson of the Grand Jury

M.P. Mickers

M. P. Mickers
District Attorney Darrow County
State of Nita 99995
(828) 555-3884

DATED: December 15, YR-1

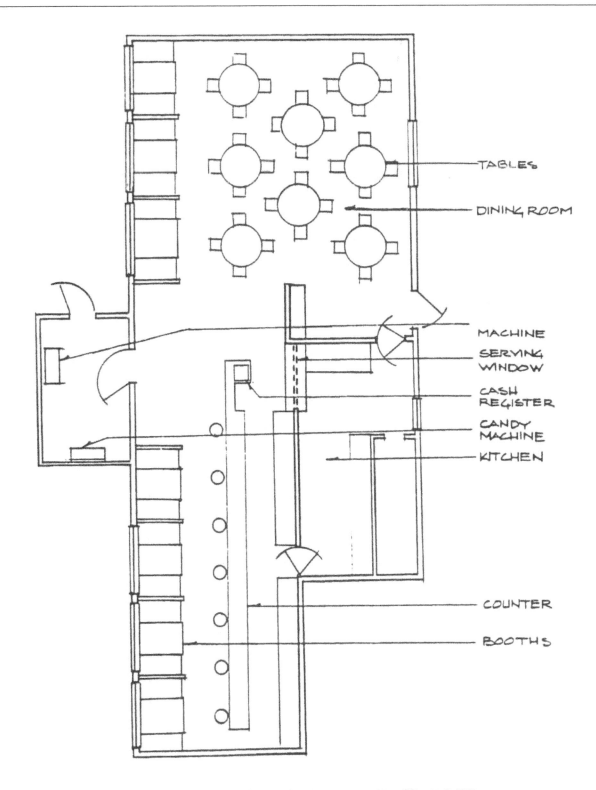

DIAGRAM OF TRUCK STOP CAFE
HIGHWAY 33, NITA CITY

(NOT DRAWN TO SCALE)

NITA CITY POLICE DEPARTMENT

OFFENSE REPORT

Re: Johnny Diamond
Location: The Truck Stop Café
                        Highway 33
                        Nita City, Nita
Offense: Homicide
Date of Report: December 9, YR-1
By: Sgt. E. A. Benbrook
                        Homicide Division

On December 1, YR-1, at about 6:55 a.m., I received a telephone call that there had been a shooting at the Truck Stop Café. I went immediately to the café. When I arrived, I met Officers Johnson and White, who also had just arrived. I instructed Officers Johnson and White to secure the scene and check for witnesses in the restaurant.

On checking the scene, I saw Johnny Diamond lying in the entranceway of the café, and Trudi Doyle was kneeling next to him, holding his hand. A handgun was by her side. There was blood on the front of his jacket, and Diamond appeared to be dead—his eyes were open, but he didn't move at all. I didn't touch the body or check to determine if Diamond was, in fact, dead.

After seeing Mr. Diamond lying there and Ms. Doyle kneeling next to him, I picked up the gun and said to Ms. Doyle, "All right, Doyle, what happened?" She didn't say anything; she just kind of stared off into space. I said, "Let's go," or something like that, and then Ms. Doyle got up. I took her to the police car, handcuffed her, and placed her in the back of the car. I told her that she was under arrest for investigation of assault, or homicide if Diamond was dead, and advised Doyle of her Miranda rights—to remain silent and to have a lawyer. (I read the rights off of our departmental card that we carry.) Doyle didn't say anything or respond at all. She just calmly sat there in the car. She looked normal and appeared to understand and know everything that was going on. I then left the car and instructed Officer White to stand at the rear of the car while I continued the investigation.

The coroner arrived and pronounced Johnny Diamond dead. His body was transferred to the County Morgue for an autopsy by Deputy Coroner Dr. Pierce.

Mr. Diamond was found lying in the entranceway to the Truck Stop Café. It is a glass-enclosed structure nine feet wide by twelve feet long (inside measurements). The lower four feet of the walls are wood, and the rest is glass. Both doors are glass. I found a package of gum (unopened) on the floor next to Mr. Diamond. The package was a box the shape of a deck of cards only thinner, and the gum was in foil that slides out of the box. I first saw it when Mr. Diamond's body was being moved out of the entranceway. The package was partially covered by Mr. Diamond's legs. There was no blood on it. Two expended cartridges were found in the northeast corner of the entranceway.

A mutilated bullet was lodged in the west wall fourteen inches to the south of the vending machine, thirty inches above the floor. I marked the cartridges with my initials, placed the cartridges and the package of gum in an evidence envelope, and then placed the envelope in an evidence locker at the station.

I spoke with Beth Kelly, who was identified by Officer Johnson as an eyewitness. Kelly told me that Ms. Doyle had gone to get gum and Mr. Diamond had intercepted her in the entranceway, that Kelly saw Ms. Doyle shake her heard "no," Mr. Diamond nod his head "yes," then two shots rang out, and Mr. Diamond slumped to the floor. At that time I didn't speak with the other two witnesses, Eric Mason (a server) and Joseph Foster (a local farmer), but simply got their names and addresses.

I checked on Ms. Doyle in the car once or twice during my investigation at the scene, and each time she was still calmly sitting in the car. I never saw her look over at Mr. Diamond, not even when the coroner came and examined Mr. Diamond. After the coroner examined Mr. Diamond, I told Ms. Doyle that Diamond was dead. She didn't respond at all, just calmly sat there like nothing had happened.

Officers Johnson and White took Ms. Doyle to the county jail, and she was booked for investigation of homicide. As part of the booking process, Ms. Doyle was tested for drugs and alcohol. This took place at approximately 1:00 p.m. These tests came back negative. After the booking process, the lab performed a neutron activation test of Ms. Doyle's hands. The results were positive. The lab also performed a neutron activation test of Johnny Diamond's hands at the morgue. Results negative.

I retained custody of the handgun that I found next to Ms. Doyle and the body of Johnny Diamond. It was a Beretta Cheetah, a.380 caliber semi-automatic pistol, serial number D 08865. When I got back to the police department, I put my initials on the gun and placed it in an evidence locker. The evidence locker is in our custodian's office. I completed the forms for the custodian. There is always a person on duty at this office, and there is a ledger or receipt for signing articles in and out. That way we have a record of where things are at all times.

Ms. Doyle gave a statement on the day of the shooting, December 1, at approximately 3:30 p.m. The statement was given in the presence of me, Officer James Anderson, and Megan Schmidt, a certified shorthand reporter.

On December 2, I checked out gun registration files and determined that the pistol had been registered to Johnny Diamond in November of YR-2. All guns have to be registered, and records are kept in the police department with a central file for the state in Capitol City.

I then examined and test fired the pistol. The gun was operable. I test fired it into a special box designed for that purpose and then recovered the bullet. I had received a bullet from Dr. Pierce, the deputy coroner, that had been recovered from the body of Mr. Diamond. I compared the two bullets by examining them under a microscope and looking at the "lands" and "grooves."

There were identical markings on both of the bullets, indicating they had been fired by the same gun. In order to be absolutely certain, I sent the bullets to the Nita State Crime Laboratory and requested their opinion. I received the bullets back with a letter, signed by Mr. Michael J. Harvey, stating that he had examined them, that they had identical markings, and it was his opinion that they had been fired from the same gun. The bullet that had been recovered from the entranceway wall was too mutilated to permit comparison.

I received special training in firearm testing and identification at the Nita State Crime Laboratory in Capitol City. This was about two years ago. I keep up-to-date on it by reading the material distributed by the Nita State Crime Laboratory and the FBI.

I submitted the jacket Diamond was wearing to the State Crime Laboratory for testing. Results for powder burns were inconclusive due to the amount of blood on the jacket. Blood type same as Diamond's. Shape of the two holes in the front of the jacket indicated that the holes were caused by bullets.

I knew Johnny Diamond when he was a police officer with our department. He was thirty years old, and a big man, over six feet tall and around 200 pounds. I first met Johnny in November YR-2, when he joined the force. I knew him fairly well, although I never worked with him. I would see him at the station quite often, and we talked about general topics. I found him pleasantly talkative, but not very revealing about his personal life. He did mention that he was married with two children, but that he has been separated from them for some time and was in the process of getting a divorce. He talked about his children a little, but never about his ex-wife. He dated some girls occasionally, but I guess they broke off the relationships. Then he met Trudi Doyle. He would talk about her, although never with any specifics. The conversation would always be general and just enough for me to know that he was with her.

I knew Ms. Doyle, but only to recognize her and know that she worked as a server at the Truck Stop Café. I didn't know anything about her personal life.

On the day Johnny Diamond was shot, December 1, I was at the station and saw Johnny Diamond. He came off duty from his shift at 5:30 a.m. I saw him as he came into the station, and he went back to his locker. As he was leaving I saw him, and we talked for a few minutes. He said that he had just resigned and that he was going to California to start over. I wished him good luck and kidded him about his love life. He said, "Well, wish me luck on that; I'm going to talk to her." I don't remember the exact words, but that was basically what he said.

When I was talking to him, I noticed that he had his "off-duty" gun in his shoulder holster. A shoulder holster fits under your jacket, so it is an easy way for a cop to carry his firearm when out of his uniform. I did notice that he never clipped the gun into the holster; I just assumed he did this so he could pull it out at a moment's notice. Johnny's shoulder holster was under his left arm, meaning he would reach it with his right hand. I saw that the hammer was back, and it was in the cocked position. I just assumed the safety was on, but I couldn't see it. It would be extremely hazardous to carry the gun cocked if the safety is off. I don't think it is unusual to carry a gun cocked with a round in the chamber, as long as the safety is on, especially for a police officer. He zipped up his jacket and left.

I talked to Diamond around 6:00 a.m. I got the call from the Truck Stop Café about the shooting around 6:50 a.m.

Submitted by:

Sgt. E.A. Benbrook
Sgt. E.A. Benbrook*
Homicide Division
Nita City Police Department

---

* Sgt. E. A. Benbrook has been a police officer with the Nita City Police Department for twelve years. He has been a sergeant for four years and has been in charge of the homicide division for two years. He is married with two children.

NITA CITY POLICE DEPARTMENT

STATEMENT OF BETH/BRIAN KELLY

My name is Beth Kelly. I am a short-order cook at the Truck Stop Café, working the day shift from 6:00 a.m. until 2:30 p.m. I live at 405½ South Fourth Street, Nita City. I am twenty-six, single, and live by myself.

I know Trudi Doyle because she worked at the Truck Stop Café with me. She also lived in a spare room in my apartment for about six months. I also knew Johnny Diamond. He used to come into the Truck Stop Café a lot, and then he began dating Trudi. Trudi is thirty-one years old and has been working as a server at the Truck Stop Café since sometime in March YR-1. She is married and has a little boy, but last I heard she was in the process of divorcing her husband. She's been separated from her husband since she came to Nita City and began working in the café. Johnny Diamond was in his late twenties, I think. He was married with two children, but was separated from his wife and children. Trudi told me that his divorce had been pending for some time.

On December 1, YR-1, I arrived at work on time, as usual. In fact, I always arrive between 5:30 and 5:45 a.m. When I walked in, I saw Trudi Doyle and two or three other servers who were coming off their shift. They went to a booth on the north side of the café and had some coffee. After a little while, I got my first order of the day, hotcakes. I remember this because when I went to the serving window to get an order, I could see Trudi get up from the booth and walk toward the front door. I turned back around and saw that she had gotten some gum from the machine and that Diamond was also standing in the entranceway, but with his back to the door. He was blocking her way back into the café. He must have been sitting in a back booth because I didn't see him get up and walk to the front.

Trudi was facing me, and Diamond was in front of her with his back toward me. Trudi had a pack of gum shaped like a box in her left hand. It was a blue and white package, the size of a deck of cards only thinner, and the gum was in a foil packet that pulls out. She had quit smoking and was using gum to keep off the cigarettes. Trudi would always go the entranceway to get candy or gum from the vending machine there.

It looked like they were about to have a fight, if you know what I mean, from the way Diamond sort of stepped in front of her to block her path to the door and by the way she shook her head "no" when he asked her something. I couldn't hear what was being said since they were in the entranceway, but I did see her shake her head "no," and he nodded his head "yes." I could see pretty well because the entranceway is glass-enclosed, and also the door is all glass. I was only fifteen feet or so away from them, the serving window being six to eight feet behind the cash register. The next thing I knew I heard two bangs; they were shots, quick like firecrackers. I heard shouts, and I thought, "Oh, God, someone's been shot." I started for the back so I could call the police.

By the time I came out to the front of the café, Johnny Diamond was lying on the floor, and Trudi was kneeling next to him holding his hand. I grabbed a wet rag from out front and went back to help revive the dishwasher. When I came back to the front of the café the police had come, and they took Trudi to the police car. I talked to Sergeant Benbrook and told him what I saw.

I had seen Diamond in the café before and knew it was him as soon as I saw him that morning on December 1. He usually came in early to have breakfast and pick up Trudi as she came off her shift.

Trudi is right-handed. I often saw her writing the orders and checks for the customers.

We are pretty good friends, and she was good company for me. Trudi had a pretty tough life, and I felt for her. Trudi grew up in a small town a little ways from Nita City. She was the youngest of four kids, and her parents were pretty poor. I guess she did really good at school, but couldn't afford to go to college, so she joined the Army after high school. She sometimes hinted that something else happened during that time, but she never told me what it was. I figured some guy broke her heart, but I don't know.

Trudi was in the Army for four years, and she used to talk a lot about the training she received there. I guess she was one of the best shots with small arms, like pistols. She always said the rifles were too big for her, but the pistols were just her size; like Annie Oakley meets Goldilocks, I guess. She never got a chance to see combat, only did clerical work in an office on the base. She said that she used to go to the shooting range twice as often as she was supposed to. She was real comfortable around guns and used to joke around a lot about them. Honestly, it sometimes made me a little nervous. I was just glad she didn't have a gun when she was living with me.

After her time in the Army, she married a guy she met on the base, and I guess it didn't go well from the start. He was a drunk and used to hit her all the time. She left him and moved to Nita City a couple years ago. She had one child, a boy around four, and she talked about him often. He is living with Trudi's mom in Capitol City, and the kid sometimes visits his dad. I guess her ex was making the divorce real ugly, fighting for custody and all of that. She worried a lot about these problems. In fact, she suffered from some pretty serious depression. When she was staying with me, I used to hear her crying in her room pretty often. I knocked a few times to see if I could help, but she never answered.

Diamond wanted to go out West, and he really wanted Trudi to go with him. But she couldn't make up her mind, and she seemed reluctant. We talked about it four or five times the last two or three days. She liked Diamond, but she didn't know if she wanted to settle down again so soon. It would be easier if he just stayed in town. She was worried about getting into another bad relationship, especially with a cop. She said that she thought she loved Diamond, but wasn't sure.

The first time I saw them together in the café that morning was when they were in the entranceway. Trudi had been sitting with the other servers before she got up to get the gum. Diamond must have been sitting someplace else by himself. She did not go talk to him—he went after her.

There were about ten to fifteen people in the café when Diamond was shot. There were a few people at the counter and some in the booths. I really don't want to talk about this anymore.

I have read the above statement consisting of three pages, and it is true and correct.

Signed: *Beth Kelly*   Date: 12/4/YR-1
            Beth Kelly

Witness: *E.A. Benbrook*   Date: 12/4/YR-1
            Sgt. E.A. Benbrook

NITA CITY POLICE DEPARTMENT

STATEMENT OF JOSEPH/JOANN FOSTER*

My name is Joseph Foster. My spouse and I run an organic farm on the outskirts of Nita City. Three or four times a week I drive my truck into town for supplies. I also come into town to run my stand at the farmer's market every Thursday. Either way, I head into town after my early morning chores and usually stop at the Truck Stop Café for breakfast. On December 1, YR-1, the day of the shooting, I had done just that and entered the café at about 6:15 or 6:20 a.m. I sat at the counter, and Mason waited on me, as usual. I ordered my hotcakes and orange juice like I do every time I'm there. I was sitting at the counter, one seat over from the cash register.

I don't know any of the other servers by name, but I noticed a group of them—three or four—sitting in a booth, far to my left, when I first walked in. The place wasn't very crowded yet, and I guess they were taking a coffee break 'till business picked up.

After ordering, I just sat there making conversation with Mason, who was busy cleaning up the counter where I was sitting. Several seconds went by, and then Johnny Diamond came tearing down the aisle to my right. He must've been sitting at one of the booths in that area of the restaurant, but I hadn't noticed him till then. He seemed to be in a big hurry and walked right past me to the front door, which I had my back to. Being curious, I tried to listen to what made Johnny pass by without saying hello. After I heard the door open, I heard what sounded like the vending machine ejecting candy or a pack of gum. I recognized that sound because I get a candy bar or a pack of gum every Monday; my spouse is trying to get me to quit smoking, so I substitute candy or gum. Can't smoke anywhere these days so might as well quit. After Johnny went into the entranceway and the glass door shut behind him, I could hear him talking to a woman, but I couldn't make out what they were saying through the door—plus it wasn't really my business. I started to say something to Mason when I heard a shot fired in the entranceway. I immediately hit the floor to my right as my combat instincts told me; I had fought in Afghanistan, and I've been spooky about sounds ever since.

---

* This statement was given to Sgt. Benbrook at Foster's farm on December 3, YR-1.

Then another shot rang out. From my military background I'd estimate it was five seconds before the second shot was fired.

I am legally blind in my left eye and have very poor vision in the right one. I lost my vision in a training accident after my service in Afghanistan. I was training some new recruits in the use of riot grenades (flash bangs), and one of the recruits dropped his grenade in the pit. The flash damaged my right eye, and some shrapnel from the casing found its way into my left eye, permanently blinding it. I was medically discharged from the Army after the grenade incident and have lived a peaceful life away from guns since my discharge. In fact, the shooting was the first time I had been near gunfire since my discharge. One nice side effect of my vision loss was that over time my other senses were heightened as I became less dependent on my eyes. This is a mixed blessing, because the coffee at the Truck Stop Café is horrible, but the pancakes are fantastic.

During my service in Afghanistan, I was a NCO in the Special Forces, with specialized training in nighttime infiltration. This training focused on the ability to judge the distance and number of troops in a patrol by the sounds they made moving through the terrain. By measuring the time in between sounds a soldier can easily know the patrol's speed, composition, and direction of travel.*

When I was sure all the shooting was finished, I got back on my feet and told Mason to call 911. I made my way over to the entranceway, but there were other people around, and I didn't want to get in the way. The people at the café said the woman was Trudi Doyle and the guy was Johnny Diamond. I'll never forget that day.

I knew Johnny Diamond for a number of years. He was a regular at my booth at the farmer's market. He always buys a couple heads of lettuce and whatever beef I have on special. Lately he has also taken to buying some flowers. I gibed him the first time he bought flowers, saying he was going soft. I remember this because my spouse told me to shut it and leave the nice young man alone. Diamond responded that he had found a good reason to go soft and was even thinking about leaving the force. I told him not to get married, but just to run off with the girl; of course my spouse hit me with some celery for that one. The last time he came to the booth, he didn't buy anything, said he was leaving

---

* Assume that women now serve in the Special Forces, both in training and in the field, so Foster may be male or female.

town and gonna take his girl with him. I wished him the best and tried to sell him some jerky for the road. I never did meet his girlfriend.

I remember all this very distinctly. After all it was the biggest thing that had happened to me in years, being an eyewitness, or I guess more of an earwitness, to a killing, that is. I'm not about to forget the details of such an experience.

I have read the above statement consisting of two pages, and it is true and correct.

Signed: *Joseph Foster*   Date: 12/3/YR-1
                   Joseph Foster

Witness: *E.A. Benbrook*   Date: 12/3/YR-1
                   Sgt. E.A. Benbrook

NITA CITY POLICE DEPARTMENT

STATEMENT OF ERIC/ESTELLE MASON*

My name is Eric Mason. I am a server at the Truck Stop Café, and I live at 502 North Allen, Nita City. I am thirty-nine years old and single. I work the day shift at the Truck Stop Café. I was there the day Johnny Diamond died.

I begin work at 6:00 a.m., which is the time the night shift ends, and my duties include waiting on customers seated at the counter. On the morning of December 1, YR-1, I arrived on time and waited on my first customer at about 6:15. The customer was Joseph Foster, a farmer who comes in several times a week around this time. I took Foster's order for hotcakes and coffee, Foster's usual. There weren't too many people in the café at that time. Foster and one other person were seated at the counter, and there were two or three booths that had people. Foster was sitting at the counter, one seat over from the cash register.

I distinctly remember seeing Officer Diamond seated at a booth not far from the counter. He came in often to pick up a server, Trudi Doyle, when her shift was over, so I thought nothing of seeing him seated there.

A little while after I had taken Foster's order (I don't know exactly what time), I saw Officer Diamond hurry past the counter toward the front door. I remember this because he was moving so quickly. I was wiping the counter area near Foster at the time, but looked up to see where Officer Diamond was going so fast. He went through the door to the entranceway where Trudi was at the vending machine. It looked like she had gotten a pack of gum or some candy. She had turned from the vending machine and was facing inside. I couldn't hear what was being said, but I could see that they were talking and that Trudi was shaking her head "no" and Officer Diamond was nodding "yes." I could see Officer Diamond was standing in the doorway. The next thing I knew, Trudi moved toward Diamond, and she made a quick movement. Diamond moved towards her quickly and kind of with a jerk. That's all I could see because his back was to me. Then I heard the sound of

---

* This statement was given to Sgt. Benbrook at the Truck Stop Café on December 5, YR-1.

a shot and a few seconds later, another one. The shots were close to one another, about one to three seconds apart. I heard Office Diamond and Trudi shout, saw him on the floor, and realized he had been shot. Foster had jumped off the seat and laid flat on the ground, I guess, when Foster heard the shots. When Foster jumped back up, Foster told me to call 911.

I immediately went to the kitchen for help and learned that someone had already called the police. When I returned to the front of the café, Trudi Doyle was kneeling over Officer Diamond, holding his hand.

The whole incident happened very fast, maybe within twenty or thirty seconds from the time I saw Officer Diamond rush past me, but it is difficult to figure such timing. I was standing only eight or ten feet from the entranceway where it happened.

I didn't see Officer Diamond's hands. I could only see his back and the upper part of Trudi's body: her head and shoulders. Officer Diamond was standing in front of her. The lower part of the entranceway is wood for about three or four feet up from the floor. Above that it's all glass.

I didn't know Trudi real well because our shifts were different, but I would talk to her most days when I was coming and she was leaving. A couple of days before the shooting, I saw her do a strange thing. She was drinking coffee and waiting for her ride after her shift, and I saw her pour something into her coffee from a small bottle. I couldn't see what it was, but she did it under the table like she was trying to be sneaky or something.

I know a lot of people think Officer Diamond is a great guy, but Diamond has always been a jerk to me. He once pulled me over because my taillight was out. I thought it would be no big deal and told him I would fix it when I could. He pulls me out of the car and makes me do all these tests like I had been drinking. I am a recovering alcoholic and haven't had a drink in three years and told him so. He wouldn't have anything to do with it. Told me people never change and once a drunk always a drunk. After I passed all his tests, he still made me blow in the stupid breathalyzer thing. Finally he let me get back in my car, but made me sit there while he ran my insurance and driver's license. Then after all of that, he still gave me a ticket for the broken taillight. The only reason I could ever figure he was mean to me was earlier that day when he had come to pick up Trudi, she and I were chatting and joking when he came in. He looked at me like he wanted to punch me just for making her laugh. He didn't say anything at the time, just grabbed Trudi's hand, and they left even though she was protesting that she wanted to hear the end of my joke.

I don't know if you are going to talk to that nutter Foster, but I should tell you Foster's crazy as a March hare. Foster's got some tall tales about being in the Army Special Forces or something, but I heard from someone way back that Foster was a supply sergeant in some back area. Who knows what's true, but I just always take what Foster says with a grain of salt. If you ask my opinion Foster's getting to the point where Foster doesn't know the truth from fiction.

I should probably tell you this, too, now that I'm thinking about it. The day before Johnny Diamond was shot, a few days after my run in with Officer Diamond over my broken taillight, Trudi came to apologize to me. Seems Officer Diamond had told her about pulling me over, and she had told him off. Trudi looked just furious when she was telling me this, shaking her fists and swearing. Trudi said she gets so mad when he gets like that, she could just kill him. I don't think she meant it; just blowing off steam.

I have read the above, and it is my statement.

Signed: *Eric Mason*   Date: 12/5/YR-1
                 Eric Mason

Witness: *E.A. Benbrook*   Date: 12/5/YR-1
                 Sgt. E.A. Benbrook

STATEMENT OF JEANNE/JOHN MADDEN*

My name is Jeanne Madden. I am a police officer in Nita City. I am thirty-two, married, with three children, and live at 481 Olive Street, Nita City. I have been a member of the Nita City Police Department for a little over nine years. I was born and raised in Nita City. I worked in my father's hardware store for a few years after high school before entering the Nita Police Academy at age twenty-two. After successfully completing police training, I became a member of the Nita City Police Department and worked my way up through the ranks until reaching my present position of sergeant.

Johnny Diamond was thirty and also lived in Nita City all his life. Although I never met Johnny until he joined the police force last year, I knew who he was, as he and my brother were about the same age and went to high school together. I, at that time, knew little about Johnny except for the fact that he had never had any police trouble.

Johnny Diamond became a member of the Nita City Police Department in November YR-2, after just having completed four years in the Marines and the usual police training. While in the Marines, he had become an expert in the use of firearms and owned a Beretta Cheetah semi-automatic pistol that he always carried while off duty.

Johnny Diamond attained a commendable record during his short time as a police officer. I was personally aware of his performance and progress since I was responsible for filing detailed quarterly reports on him. Johnny Diamond was competent in all aspects of police work and displayed a good attitude toward his work.

In Nita City, we encourage, but do not require, all police officers to carry a loaded firearm while off duty. This is written right in the Nita City Police Department Duty Manual. Carrying the weapon in this way enables officers to better carry out their sworn affirmative duty to enforce the law twenty-four hours a day. It has been our experience that unarmed, off-duty officers are sometimes unable to effectively fulfill that duty when faced with certain emergency situations.

---

* This statement was given to John DeGroff, investigator for defense counsel, at Madden's home on December 6, YR-1.

It is my understanding that Officer Diamond was carrying his off-duty weapon immediately after having resigned from the force on December 1 and that this instrument caused the death of Johnny Diamond less than an hour after he went off duty that day.

I am familiar with the Cheetah semi-automatic. Several of our officers have such a weapon; also I'm used to carrying that kind of gun myself. It was my practice to carry the gun with the hammer in the uncocked position with a bullet in the firing chamber. In my opinion, this is the best way for a police officer to carry this gun because with a round in the chamber, it is ready to be used in case of an emergency. It is also very safe because the safety is on, and there is little chance the gun will go off accidentally.

Johnny Diamond and I both worked the night shift (9:00 p.m. to 5:30 a.m.). As I was responsible for familiarizing the new officers with their duties, Johnny Diamond and I occasionally worked together on an assignment or patrol beat. We became friendly with one another, but not to the extent where we socialized outside of work. Also, our outside interests were perhaps divergent, as I am married with three children, and he is separated from his wife.

Having worked with Diamond for several months, I got to know him quite well, both professionally and personally. He was a good officer and an excellent person to work with. Occasionally we would talk about our personal lives, and I knew that he was married with two children, but he had been separated from his wife and children. His divorce had been pending since January YR-1. He began dating Trudi Doyle sometime in late September YR-1, and they had lived together for a couple of months before Johnny's death on December 1, YR-1. Diamond seemed so much happier after he met Trudi Doyle. He was excited about life and looking forward to the future. Although I didn't personally know Ms. Doyle, I had seen her a couple of times at the Truck Stop Café, where she worked as a server. That particular diner was a favorite coffee-break spot for several police officers.

During the night of November 27, YR-1 (four days before Diamond was shot), Diamond and I were on patrol duty together. It was at that time that Diamond first told me of his decision to resign from the police force and move to California. Diamond said that he loved Trudi and wanted to take her to California with him because of her dissatisfaction with Nita City and her depressed state of mind. Diamond then told me about what had happened with Trudi just a day or so before. Apparently Trudi had attempted to commit suicide by taking an overdose of barbiturates and that Diamond arrived home just in time to save her life by inducing vomiting and taking her to the hospital. Diamond also told me that she at one other time had unsuccessfully attempted suicide with aspirin.

After Trudi's latest suicide attempt, Diamond said that he got really worried about Trudi and knew he had to shock her into reality in order to cure her of her inclination to kill herself. To impress on Trudi the seriousness of her act, Diamond pointed to his unloaded pistol and said, "If anyone is going to kill you, I am." This happened the afternoon that Diamond took Trudi home from the hospital. Diamond was very worried about Trudi's depressed condition, and he thought maybe that would shock her out of it and make her realize the seriousness and stark reality of her suicide attempts.

Diamond also told me that Trudi had not yet made up her mind to go to California with him, but that he would leave with or without her because he wanted to get away from life in Nita City.

After his shift ended that night (morning of November 28), Diamond submitted his resignation to become effective December 1, YR-1.

On the day of December 1, Diamond completed his normal shift at 5:30 a.m., and he left his forwarding address with the desk clerk, so his paycheck would be sent to him. Diamond was shot in the Truck Stop Café at around 6:30 a.m. that morning, but I know little more than that both Diamond and Doyle were present at the scene of the shooting when the police arrived and that Doyle did not resist arrest. I was at home and asleep at the time of the shooting.

I would like to go on the record again as stating that Johnny was a fine officer of the law and had received several commendations for superior duty. I have read the above, and it is my statement.

Signed: *J. Madden*   Date: 12/6/YR-1
Sgt. J. Madden

Witness: **John DeGroff**   Date: 12/6/YR-1
John DeGroff

Memo from Sgt. Benbrook

Date: December 10, YR-1

To: Diamond homicide file

From: Sgt. E.A. Benbrook

Subject: Diamond's laptop retrieved from Diamond's car, contained a recent email to his mom

Diamond's vehicle was found outside the Truck Stop Café and impounded. Personal effects found in vehicle were taken to headquarters, cataloged, and filed. Of interest to the homicide investigation is a draft of an email from Diamond to his mom that was found in the drafts section of Diamond's Gmail account. The draft had a computer date and time of 11:30 p.m. the night before Diamond was shot at Truck Stop Café.

Text of the draft email follows:

"Send by email when on the road to California.

Hi Mom: Sorry I've been out of touch for a while. I hope this finds you well. So much has been going on lately I hardly know where to start. Guess it's best to just jump in with the latest and work my way back.

First off, I should tell you I gave notice at work a few days ago. As of December 1, your son will no longer be a Nita City police officer. I really just want to move to California with my girlfriend Trudi, and once I'd made the decision, I didn't want to wait anymore, so I gave notice on November 28 and told my boss, Sgt. Madden, that my last day would be at the end of my shift on December 1. I told him I wanted to move to California and hopefully marry Trudi, but that even if Trudi turns me down, it was just time for me to leave Nita City.

Why California, you ask? Time for a big change, time for a new life. Not just for me, but for Trudi, too, I hope. I know I haven't said much about her to you yet, Mom, but I want you to know everything. Trudi and I haven't been together long, just a few months, but for me it's long enough to know I love her and want to be with her. I've already asked her to marry me just as soon as our divorces come through. She says she loves me, too.

We met at the restaurant she works at, the Truck Stop Café, on the edge of town. We met in late September, and she moved into my place about a month ago. We both work the night shift, so we have our days open to spend together, and we just have a lot in common. Trudi was in the Army before she got married and is an experienced marksman – well, markswoman, actually! She was trained on the Beretta 92fs, a standard issue, semi-automatic handgun. I have a.380 Beretta Cheetah as well as my service pistol, and always carry one or the other on my person when I'm off-duty, just as most Nita City cops do. (We cops don't want to be caught helpless in an emergency.) But seeing how good Trudi was at shooting practice made me want her to have my Cheetah, so after a few months together, I gave it to her as a present. She was pretty excited about that, and she used it when we'd go to shooting practice together.

There are always a lot of guys who hassle Trudi at work—truck drivers and traveling salesmen hitting on her and stuff. She's petite, so I guess they think they can get away with it. One creep in particular has been after her with coarse language and making passes at her, so that's part of why I wanted her to have the gun. I've also been teaching her judo. She likes trying to snatch my gun off me when I'm off duty and have it holstered. It's like a game for her, figuring out how to defend herself and disarm an attacker. That's why I always take the rounds out of my pistol when I'm with her. If she tries to disarm me, I don't want it to accidentally discharge.

So, that's the good stuff about Trudi. As I sort of hinted at, she's still married, just like I am. She's separated though. Her husband is nothing but trouble; they were in the Army together, but the marriage is over. There's also a moodiness and sadness about her that worries me. Maybe it's depression. I wouldn't be surprised. Her childhood was pretty tough. Her dad was in and out of work a lot, so her family didn't have much money. She's told me that if she could've gone to college, her life would've turned out a lot different. Instead, she joined the Army, met her jerk husband, which didn't help, and things've just stayed kind of hard for her. Anyone would get depressed under those circumstances, I think. But when she's feeling good, Trudi is such a joy to be around! Her future feels bright when she's happy, but when she's in a funk, everything in life is a real struggle for her.

And that brings me to the really bad part. Trudi took an overdose of sleeping pills the other day, just two days before I resigned from the police force. On November 26, I came home in the afternoon and found her in that state, so I force-fed her some milk and olive oil and made her throw up the sleeping pills. Then I took her to the hospital to have her stomach pumped. They kept her overnight for observation. I wasn't on duty that night, so I stayed the night at the hospital with her. That's when she told me that she'd tried to kill herself once before, back before I met her. She'd OD'd on aspirin, but all that did was make her feel sick and cause ringing in her ears. I'm glad she was ok that time and again this time, but I have to admit that I'm really concerned about her. Having given her that Cheetah suddenly seemed like a terrible idea, given her emotional state, so after she fell asleep again, I ran back home to find the gun and hide it from her. I ended up taking it to work with me on my next work shift and stowing it in my locker for safekeeping.

So, anyway. She was still sleeping when I got back to the hospital, and because I was so worried about her after realizing she'd tried to kill herself before, I did something I know I shouldn't have—but I just couldn't help it. I looked at her medical chart. I know it's private and I shouldn't have, but I just wanted to get a sense of what her doctors thought. So, I looked. Who wouldn't? Well, I learned a few more shocking things about her, namely that she'd been raped right out of high school and had an abortion because of it. Mom, between that and the news of the first suicide attempt, I realized how truly difficult her life had been and that I needed to help her through it. That's when I decided we should go to California together and start over.

So when Trudi woke up the next morning, I told her I wanted us to leave for California ASAP and start a new life together. She promised to think it over, but she didn't exactly commit herself to going. She was released from the hospital that afternoon, and I drove her home. In order to frighten her and help her realize how serious and stupid she was being with her life, I pointed to the pistol, which

I knew was unloaded. I told her how strong she was. How she had survived so much: two suicide attempts, being raped, having an abortion. I told her that she was strong enough to not only live, but to learn to love life again. I told her that life, our life together, was worth living. Then, to shock her back into reality, I said, "If anybody's going to kill you, it will be me." She didn't say a word. She just stared back at me. I didn't recognize the look in her eyes, but it definitely wasn't fear. I don't know what it was....... Mom, it is really late, i need to get some sleep before i take off tomorrow. I'll finish it and send when I'm on the road – hope Trudi is with me and we both get a fresh start in life."

Sgt. E.A. Benbrook
December 10, YR-1

Nita City Police Department

Statement of Trudi Doyle*

This statement was given by Trudi Doyle at the Nita City Police Station between 3:30 and 4:00 p.m. on December 1, YR-1. The statement was transcribed stenographically in the presence of Sgt. E. A. Benbrook, Officer James Anderson, and the shorthand reporter, Megan Schmidt.

By Doyle:

Yes, I know I've been charged with the first-degree murder of my boyfriend, Johnny Diamond.

I was born and grew up in Nita City. I am twenty-seven years old, my birthday is October 18, YR-28. I was married and have one child. I filed for divorce in November YR-3, and it became final in June YR-2.

Our family was dirt poor—father had work on and off and mom was an alcoholic and couldn't keep a job. I was the oldest of four children, two younger brothers and a girl was the baby of the family. I did very well in high school, but couldn't afford to go to college. I worked at minimum wage jobs and it became obvious I had no future in Nita City other than getting knocked up and ending up in a life like my parents.

In October YR-9, when I was nineteen, I left Nita City to join the Army. I received some good training in the Army in terms of handling firearms and war stuff, but nothing useful for the outside world. I left the Army with an honorable discharge in October YR-3, when I was twenty-three. I came back to Nita City in June YR-2.

I got married in June YR-5 when I was twenty-three and he was twenty-eight or twenty-nine. I met my husband in the Army—he was an enlisted man who had been in the Army since high school. The first year of our marriage was fine because my husband was deployed overseas except for a week

* This statement was taken while the defendant, Trudi Doyle, was in custody on a charge of murder and without having been advised of her right to remain silent and to have an attorney. The statement may **not** be used by the prosecution during its case-in-chief, but it may be used for impeachment if the defendant testifies. *Harris v. New York*, 401 U.S. 222 (1971).

stateside. When my husband came back from that deployment, about a year after we got married, I got pregnant, and I then realized he was an alcoholic. Memories of my mom and what happened to her life haunted me. My son was born in May YR-3, in an Army hospital. Within two months I knew my son and I couldn't stay with my husband. He was verbally abusive from the time he came home after the first deployment, and then after my son was born he pushed me around and hit me a couple of times. I went to see the chaplain at the base, got some counseling, and decided to file for divorce and to get out of the Army. I petitioned the Army for a separation from my husband, which was granted, and my son and I got separate living quarters. I waited to file for divorce until after I left the Army. I left the Army in October YR-3 and filed for divorce in November YR-3.

On leaving the Army in October YR-3, I went to Capitol City and lived with my brother, his wife, and one child. Filed with the Army for child support from my ex-husband, and that got caught up in paper work. Living with my brother lasted a couple of months, and I knew it wasn't a long-term solution. Soon after moving in with my brother, I got a minimum wage job, and within two months I had saved enough to make a deposit on a one-bedroom apartment. Child care ate up all my money, and soon I knew that wouldn't work. In July YR-2, I moved back to Nita City. Still no child support from my ex as it was tied up in paper work. I got a job as a server at the Truck Stop Café, but couldn't make enough to pay for child care. My brother and his wonderful wife offered to take my son until I got settled with a better job. In September, YR-2 I got a room with a friend (Kelly). I took a couple of days off and moved my son to my mom's place in Capitol City. I planned to save money until I could get a better job and get my son back.

I began dating Johnny Diamond in late September YR-1, about two months before his death. Johnny was a local police officer. Johnny and I worked the night shift, so we had a lot of time to spend with each other during the day. Johnny said that he was in love with me and asked me to marry him as soon as his divorce was final. I wasn't sure what to do—the memory of my first marriage, my mom, and my responsibilities to my son kept haunting me. I liked Johnny a lot, but worried about it being too quick, like my first marriage, and I really didn't know much about Johnny.

We lived together at Johnny's place for about a month before December 1. Johnny knew a lot about judo from his days as a Marine and so he spent time teaching me to defend myself and how to disarm an assailant. I really enjoyed those lessons. We made them into games, and Johnny was fun to be with—patient and never abusive like my first husband. I particularly enjoyed trying to snatch Johnny's gun from his holster whenever we were off duty and horsing around. Johnny always removed all the bullets from his pistol when we horsing around so it wouldn't accidentally discharge.

Johnny constantly carried a gun, whether on or off duty; Johnny told me that police officers in Nita City were encouraged, though not required, to be armed while off duty so that they would not be helpless in an emergency situation. Johnny's personal pistol was a.380 Beretta Cheetah that he carried when off duty. I'm not sure what his service pistol was.

Johnny told me that he was a police officer with the Nita City Police Department from November YR-2 to December YR-1. Before that, Johnny had been in the Marines for six years after having bounced from job to job with no particular career goals. Johnny said that the Marines really helped to straighten him out in terms of life goals and handling responsibility. Johnny wanted to settle down and have a real family—or so he told me. Oh, one other thing Johnny told me was that he got an Honorable Discharge and was awarded a Purple Heart while fighting in Afghanistan. No, I never saw his discharge papers or the Purple Heart; I didn't even think to ask for them.

I had a lot of experience with guns myself. In the Army I received training on the Beretta 92fs semi-automatic pistol. The Cheetah is the smaller version of that standard-issue pistol. After Johnny and I had been dating for a while, he gave me the Cheetah as a present. I used it when we would go shooting together.

I was interested in the judo lessons Johnny gave me because I am a small woman and I'm around some rough and tough guys at the Truck Stop Café and when I go out. Johnny told me he wanted me to have the Cheetah because of the incidents I had told him about.

Yes, I've struggled with depression; you must have talked with Kelly. I had a tough life growing up, and marrying my first husband when I was in the Army didn't help. In fact, his verbal and physical abuse dragged me down a lot. Then when I couldn't keep my son, it was too much.

I did try to commit suicide—once half-heartedly with aspirins, which resulted in my getting sick with a terrible headache and a ringing sensation in my ears. The second time was while I was dating

Johnny. On November 26, I was home alone, and around noon I got a note from my brother that my son was in preschool and doing real well. Didn't say a word about his missing me. I felt like a terrible person, a worthless mother, and got really depressed. I took some sleeping pills, didn't work, and took some more. Next thing I know I am in the hospital. At the hospital they pumped my stomach and held me overnight. Johnny came to the hospital and was very kind and helpful. Made me feel like living.

Johnny was at the hospital all night and took me to his place the next day. Johnny told me he was so worried about me that he found the Cheetah gun he had given me and took it with him to work. The next morning while we were still at the hospital, Johnny told me that he was taking his Cheetah pistol back; didn't want me to have it; he told me several times that he really wanted me to go to California with him.

Johnny drove me home from the hospital, and while driving home, Johnny talked about how stupid it was for me to try to kill myself, that I had a lot to live for, and that I was a strong and resilient person. Johnny kept telling me how strong I had been in my life, how I have survived so much, and that I could learn to love life, and that we could do it together.

While driving me home, Johnny pointed to the Cheetah pistol, which I knew was always unloaded around me, and told me something like, "If anybody's going to kill you, it will be me." I didn't say anything or respond because I knew Johnny was trying to show me how much he cared about me and how much I had to live for.

So you got my medical records from the hospital. Yes, I was sexually assaulted while in basic training in the Army. I got pregnant, and it was either a discharge or an abortion—so I got an abortion. Couldn't report the sexual assault because they would just blame the woman, cover it up, and harass me. I went to see an Army counsellor and was advised to keep it quiet and if I got pregnant to get an abortion. About a year later, I met my husband and everything was fine while he was deployed overseas. He came back, I got pregnant, and things went downhill. No wonder I got depressed.

On December 1, I worked my usual night shift, and around six o'clock that morning I sat down to have breakfast and chat with a couple of other servers. I didn't see Johnny come in. In fact, I didn't know he was there until we were both in the entranceway. I'm trying to quit smoking, so I went to the entranceway to get a pack of gum. The entranceway is between the door to the street and another door leading into the restaurant area itself. This latter door is glass, and it shut behind Johnny, so I doubt anyone could hear what was being said. Also, Johnny's back was to the restaurant, so anyone looking in would have a hard time seeing what was happening.

Johnny asked me to go to California with him; he was leaving that morning. I told him I needed more time, I couldn't just leave so quickly. It wasn't reasonable for me to leave my son like that. I told Johnny we needed more time together to get to know each other better.

Then, it looked like he was reaching for the Cheetah in his holster. We both grabbed for the pistol, and then next thing I knew the gun went off and a few seconds later a second shot. I didn't feel anything, but Johnny yelled, and I saw blood on his jacket. Johnny slumped to the ground, and I screamed.

Johnny was on the floor of the entranceway, and I knelt beside him, holding his hand. Johnny mumbled something I couldn't understand; I told him I loved him and I was sorry. The next thing I knew, the police arrived, and I went with them without resistance. I didn't talk to the police at first, because I was too stunned and shocked at what had happened. Later I got a lawyer, and he told me not to say anything to the police at all.

The police told me the Cheetah was cocked before it was fired; Johnny must have done that because I didn't. Johnny told me that he and most of the other officers carried their gun with it cocked and the safety on. He said it is perfectly safe to do that as long as the safety is on.

I can't believe what happened. The only person who has cared for me is now gone, and he died by the pistol he gave me for my protection. This has been a terrible and traumatic experience for me, and I can't talk about it anymore right now.

I hereby certify that this is a true and correct transcription of the statement made by Trudi Doyle on December 1, YR-1, at the Nita City Police Station.

Certified by

Megan Schmidt

Megan Schmidt

Certified Shorthand Reporter (CSR)

OFFICE OF THE CORONER
DARROW COUNTY
NITA CITY, NITA 99995

December 3, YR-1

Sgt. E. A. Benbrook
Homicide Division
Nita City Police Department
Nita City, Nita

RE: Deceased Johnny Diamond
DOD: 12-1-YR-1

Dear Sgt. Benbrook:

Enclosed is a copy of the autopsy report for Mr. Johnny Diamond. There were five entry and exit bullet wounds: entry and exit wound on the right wrist; two entry wounds and one exit wound on the upper torso. The paths of the bullets in the upper torso were on a downward angle. A diagram reconstructing the entry, exit, and path of the bullets is appended to the autopsy report.

One bullet was recovered. It was placed in an evidence container that was sealed and marked with my initials. It will be sent to you by messenger, unless I receive other instructions.

Generally, my medical background is medical school, general internship, and residency in pathology at the Nita Medical Center. I am a board-certified pathologist, and my practice is limited to pathology. I completed my residency in YR-7, and I have been board certified since YR-5. I am presently a Deputy Coroner, and I have been with the office since YR-7.

If either your office or the prosecuting attorney desires further information in this regard, please contact me.

Sincerely,

Jamie Pierce
Jamie Pierce, MD
Deputy Coroner

JP:ns
Enclosure

Department of the Medical Examiner
Nita City

HC 8205

Case Title____In Re Doyle, Nita City Police Department_____

Pathologist____Jamie Pierce, MD_____Autopsy No.__6172_____

Physician_____Darrow County Coroner, Nita City, Nita____Hospital No. NA_____

Patient Johnny Diamond_____Age 30_____Sex M_____ Race_W_____

Date, Hour–Death 12/1/YR-1_____Autopsy 12/1/YR-1, 10 a.m. M.E. No._1-2315_____

Mortuary_____Darrow County Morgue_____

Clinical Data

At 7:10 a.m. on December 1, YR-1, the Coroner's Office was informed of a shooting death and instructed to proceed to the Truck Stop Café in Nita City, Nita, to obtain the body for autopsy. A person identified as Johnny Diamond, male, was found in the entranceway of the Truck Stop Café. Diamond was dead, and the body was transferred to the county morgue at approximately 7:30 a.m. by Coroner's Office personnel.

I began the postmortem examination at 10:00 a.m. Lateral and AP x-rays of the chest were taken prior to the autopsy; labeled with the date, autopsy number, and the letters "TD"; and then preserved. These were interpreted to show a solitary radiodense foreign body in the region of the right paraspinous musculature. Significant cardiomegaly was also noted.

Officer Smith (Nita City Police Department) was present during the postmortem examination. Postmortem photographs were taken by Officer Smith and Dr. Pierce.

Diagnoses

1. Gunshot wound to the right wrist.
2. Gunshot wound to the right anterior thorax.
3. Gunshot wound to the left anterior thorax.

Cause of Death

Massive right hemothorax secondary to gunshot wounds of the chest.

Postmortem Examination

General External Appearance

The body is that of a young adult Caucasian man who measures sixty-four seventy-four inches in length, weighs 210 pounds, and appears to be approximately the stated age. Postmortem rigidity is present in the muscles of mastication at the time of autopsy. Postmortem lividity is present posteriorly and is not fixed.

The arm span (reach) is 76 inches.

General external appearance of the anterior and posterior thorax, anterior abdominal wall and flanks is normal.

General external appearance of the extremities is normal.

Clothing

The body was dressed in the following articles of clothing that were removed without alteration and labeled with the autopsy number, date, and letters JD: tan outer coat, blue shirt, blue jeans, black underwear, black socks and black shoes, rubber soles.

The tan outer coat is soaked with liquid and dried blood, and on each side of the midline of the frontal portion there is an approximately circular 8 mm in diameter hole. The fabric at the margins of these holes is frayed, but not charred, and powder residue cannot be found at the periphery of these holes with the unaided eye.

A battery watch with a damaged metal wrist band is worn on the decedent's right wrist. The watch has the correct time and is running.

External Injury

There is an approximately rectangular 1 by 0.8 cm wound on the external surface of the right wrist, centered at a point 1 cm medial and 1 cm proximal to the ulnar head. There is no evidence of powder deposition, stippling, or burning at the margins of this wound, but fragments of metal, similar in color and consistency, were found along the subcutaneous tract. This wound is consistent with a gunshot wound of entrance with an overlying intermediary target and is designated for purposes of reference as wound #1.

There is a "punched-out," irregularly margined, approximately circular 9 mm in diameter wound on the volar surface of the right wrist. There is a 2 mm abrasion collar at the margins of this wound, and no evidence of powder stippling, burning, or soot at the periphery of the wound. This wound is consistent with a shored wound of exit, and is designated as wound #2. The metal wrist band worn by the decedent does not overlie the volar tract of this wound.

There is an approximately 8 mm in diameter wound in the skin of the right anterior thorax, centered at a point 15 cm cephalad to the manubrial notch and 4.5 cm right lateral to the midline. A concentric

4 mm wide abrasion ring is at the periphery of this wound, and a 1 by 1 mm metallic foreign body, similar in color and consistency to that of the metal wrist band worn by the decedent, is embedded in the skin of the abrasion collar. There is no evidence of soot deposition, stippling, or burning at the margins or subcutaneous depths of this wound, which for purposes of reference is arbitrarily designated as wound #3.

There is an approximately circular 8 mm in diameter wound in the skin of the left anterior thorax, centered at a point 15 cm cephalad to the manubrial notch and 5 cm left lateral to the midline. A 2 mm wide abrasion collar is at the margin of this wound, and there is no evidence of burning, stippling, or soot deposition at the periphery or subcutaneous depths of the wound. For purposes of reference, this wound is arbitrarily designated as wound #4.

There is a 1 cm laceration in the skin of the right posterior thorax, centered at a point 20 cm caudad to the lowest crease of the neck and 3 cm right lateral to the midline. There is no evidence of marginal abrasion at the periphery of this wound. This wound is consistent with a gunshot wound of exit and this wound is arbitrarily designated as wound #5.

There are no other external injuries.

Internal Examination

The subcutaneous fat of the abdomen is 1 to 1.5 cm thick, and the subcutaneous fat of the thorax is approximately 1 cm thick. Each of the abdominal organs is present and is located in its normal anatomical situs. The peritoneal surfaces are smooth and glistening. The left subdiaphragmatic space contains approximately 15 cc of clotted and nonclotted blood.

The right chest cavity contains approximately 2000 cc of clotted and nonclotted blood. The left chest cavity contains approximately 25 cc of straw-colored serous fluid.

Internal Injury

A tract is followed from the wound on the extensor surface of the right wrist through the subcutaneous fat, interosseous ligament, and tendon of the palmaris longus muscle. It exits through the wound on the volar surface of the wrist. Major arteries, veins, and nerves are not involved within the tract of this wound.

A tract, which for purposes of reference is arbitrarily designated as tract A, is followed from wound #3 in the right anterior thorax through the space between the fifth and sixth costal cartilage, into the pericardial sac and through the epicardium, myocardium, and endocardium of the anterior then posterior walls of the right ventricle, exiting the posterior portion of the pericardial sac into a laceration of the right branch of the pulmonary artery and right mainstem bronchus, through the parenchyma of the right middle lobe and into the space between the third and fourth ribs posteriorly, and into the right paraspinous musculature. A severely distorted metal projectile is removed from the terminal point of this tract and is placed in a labeled bullet envelope.

There is approximately 2000 cc of clotted and nonclotted blood within the right chest cavity, as described above, and in addition there is hemorrhage along the tract of this wound from the point of entrance in the right anterior thorax to the point of termination in the right paraspinous musculature. Approximately 500 cc of blood was found in the pericardial sac, which is a finding in cardiac tamponade.

The trajectory of this tract (A) makes an angle of approximately 5 degrees to a sagittal plane and 15 degrees caudad to a transverse plane, which is slightly downward when measured from the front to the back of the decedent.

A tract, which for purposes of reference is arbitrarily designated as tract B, is followed from wound #4 in the left anterior thorax through the left anterior thorax through the costal cartilage of the sixth and seventh ribs, though the dome of the left hemidiaphragm and into the inferiormost portion of the pericardial sac without involvement of the heart itself, across the midline and into the dome of the right hemidiaphragm, into the inferiormost portion of the right of the right chest cavity and a 1 by 6 cm laceration of the anterobasal segment of the right upper lung lobe, into a 1 cm wound of the posterior parietal pleura between the fifth and sixth ribs, into the right paraspinous musculature and through the exit wound #5 in the right posterior thorax.

The trajectory of this tract (B) makes an angle of approximately 30 degrees medial to a sagittal plane and 10 degrees caudad to a transverse plane, which is downward and from the left to right when measured from the front to the back to the decedent.

There are no other internal injuries.

Respiratory System

The right lung has a mass of 250 grams and is collapsed. The left lung has a mass of 325 grams and is fully expanded. The pulmonary artery segments are normal, except as described above. The segmental and subsegmental bronchi contain approximately 15 to 20 cc of liquid and dried blood, but are otherwise normal. The parenchyma of the left lung is normal. The cut surfaces of the right lung are normal except for atelectasis.

Cardiovascular System

The heart has a mass of 280 grams. The cardiac valves are thin and pliable, and the coronary arteries are free of atheromatous plaque formation.

The tunneling tract of the projectile through the anterior and posterior walls of the right ventricle created a cardiac tamponade where the normally potential space between the pericardium and heart muscle is filled with blood. The right ventricular wall is 3 mm thick, and the left ventricular wall is 11 mm thick. The myocardium has a uniform red-brown color and is normal.

The thoracic and abdominal portions of the aorta are normal.

Hepatobiliary System

The gall bladder wall is thin and pliable and the lumen contains approximately 25 cc of green-black bile and no stones. The parenchyma is firm and has areas of nodularity. Notably, the liver tissue is not uniformly brown in color and has areas of scarring.

The liver has a mass of 1260 grams; the capsule of the liver is intact, except for the diaphragmatic reflection of the right lobe. The parenchyma is firm and has a uniform tan-brown color.

Lymphoid System

Para-aortic, hilar, and para-tracheal lymph nodes are small and appear normal.

The spleen has a mass of 110 grams. The capsule is intact, and the red pulp is firm. Lymphoid tissue is easily discernible and is represented by uniform 0.5 mm in diameter aggregates of gray-white tissue scattered throughout the parenchyma.

Pancreas and Adrenals

The pancreas and adrenals are normal.

Genitourinary System

Each kidney has a mass of 120 grams. The capsules of the kidneys are intact and the corticomedullary injunctions are distinct. The pelves and ureters are normal.

The bladder contains approximately 150 cc of clear yellow urine. The bladder mucosa is normal.

Gastrointestinal System

The esophageal and gastric mucosa are intact. The stomach contains approximately 300 cc of incompletely digested particulate food matter.

The small intestine, appendix, and large bowel are normal.

Brain and Central Nervous System

The calvarium is of average thickness, and there is no evidence of subgaleal, subdural, or subarachnoid hemorrhage.

The brain has a mass of 1280 grams. The gyri of the cerebral hemispheres are normally prominent, and the sulci are normally narrow. Serial coronal sections of the cerebrum and serial transverse sections of the cerebrum and serial transverse sections of the cerebellum are normal. The midbrain, pons, and medulla are normal.

Neck Structures

The hyoid bone and thyroid cartilage are intact.

The lobes of the thyroid gland have approximately equal mass and have a uniform bright red-brown color and a normal firm texture. Parathyroid tissue is difficult to isolate, and none is found.

The cervical portion of the esophageal mucosa is normal.

The larynx and main stem bronchi contain aspirated blood, as described above.

Toxicology

For purposes of a blood alcohol determination, blood is aspirated from the left atrium of the heart during performance of the postmortem examination. An aliquot of urine, a portion of liver, and the gastric contests are also saved.

Comment

Microscopic examination will not be performed at this time. However, representative portions of each organ will be embedded in paraffin and will be available for microscopic examination if it becomes necessary at a future date.

Addendum

The postmortem blood alcohol level is 0.008 g/dL. Postmortem vitreous chemistries are within normal limits.

Jamie Pierce

Jamie Pierce, MD
Deputy Coroner
Darrow County
Nita City, Nita 99995

Dictated 12-1-YR-1 Signed 12-3-YR-1

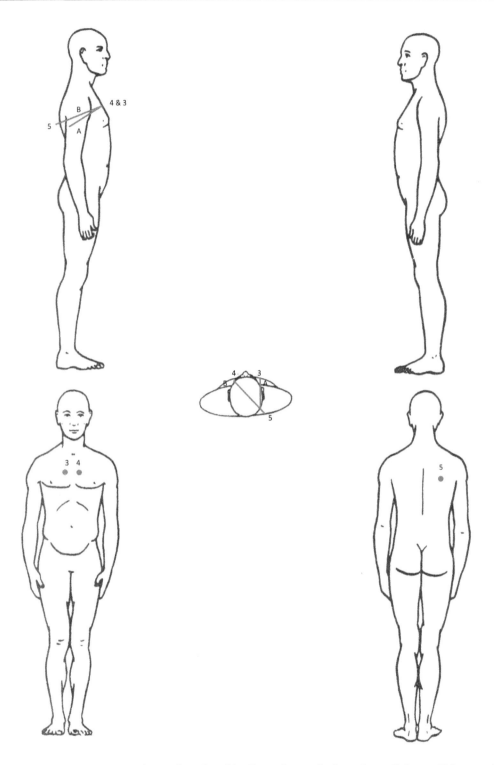

Diagram reconstructing entry, exit, and path of bullets through decedent, Johnny Diamond.

Jamie Pierce

Jamie Pierce, MD
Deputy Coroner

Memorial Hospital Report: Emergency Room Treatment No. 04535	Name	First Trudi		Middle Ann			Last Doyle	
	Sex F	Age 27	Date of Admission 11/26/YR-1	Time of Admission 3:20 p.m.		Date of Discharge 11/27/YR-1	Time of Discharge 3:00 p.m.	
	Address Street 1243 Maple Lane			City Nita City			State NI	Zip 99995
	Telephone Number (828) 555-0979		Brought in by P.O. John Diamond			Relationship		

Insurance Provider Blue Cross		Policy Number 663392559		Group Number 001-555-972		
Employer Truck Stop Cafe	Employer Phone (828) 555-3266	Employer Address Street Highway 33		City Nita City	State NI	Zip 99995
Vital Signs B.P. 100/55 P. 43 T. 98.6 R. 12	Examining Physician K. Troyer, MD		Family Doctor W. Raycoff, MD		Nurse's Initials S.J.	
	☐ X-Ray	☐ EKG	☐ Lab	☐ Pharm	☐ M & S	

Allergies

History
Patient swallowed bottle of Nembutal. Unknown no. of pills.
Had been very depressed the last week.
Prior surgeries: abortion, YR-9, after sexual assault.

Exam
Patient semi-comatose. Responds poorly to pain stimulae. Voice, speech slurred. Respiration slow and shallow. Pulse poor quality. Temp. normal. No outward sign of head injury. Pupils round, regular, equal.

Treatment
Stomach pumped. Blood barbit. level drawn.

Diagnosis
Barbituate poisoning.

Disposition of Patient Held	Referred to:	DL	Hospital X	Home	Other:	Condition of Patient on Discharge recovered

Certified as a true and correct copy of the original in the medical files of Memorial Hospital.

William Coleman

William Coleman
Medical Record Librarian

Diagram of Beretta 84FS Cheetah Semi-Automatic
(hand drawn by Sgt. Benbrook)

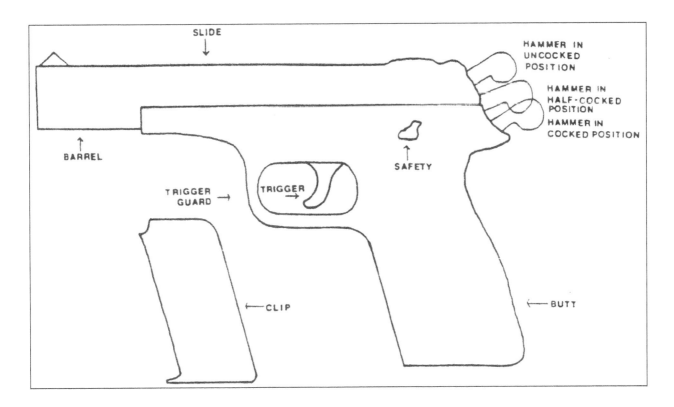

Beretta 84FS Cheetah (Labeled)

1) Barrel
2) Open slide design
3) Firing pin block (prevents pistol from firing if dropped)
4) Sights
5) Ambidextrous safety (accommodates right- and left-handed shooters)
6) Reversible magazine release (accommodates right- and left-handed shooters)
7) Anodized alloy frame
8) Trigger guard
9) Double-action trigger

Thirteen- or ten-round magazines

Operation of Beretta 84FS Cheetah Semi-Automatic

1. Bullets are placed in the magazine. This model's magazine holds thirteen rounds.

2. The magazine is inserted in the end of the butt of the gun.

3. A bullet is inserted into the firing chamber. This procedure, called chambering a round, is performed by pulling back and releasing the slide. This also cocks the hammer, thus readying the gun to fire.

4. When a round is chambered and the hammer cocked, the gun may be placed in an uncocked position by manipulating the safety/de-cocker lever.

5. When the magazine is loaded and the pistol is fired, the gas behind the exiting bullet forces the slide mechanism back, thus automatically ejecting the spent shell, forcing the hammer back into the cocked position and, while sliding forward again, chambering a new bullet. The pistol is then ready to be fired again by merely pulling the trigger.

6. Because this gun will not be actually loaded or fired in courtroom demonstrations, the chambering of the each round between pulling the trigger must be performed manually, as described in paragraph 3.

7. The safety is a small catch that when released will prevent the gun from firing even though it is cocked. It must be released manually.

8. The pistol may also fire with the hammer down, in double-action mode (like a revolver). The trigger pull is substantially heavier in the double-action mode.

Beretta Cheetah 84FS Specifications

Caliber: .380 caliber

Action: Double or Single Action

Overall Length: 6.77 inches

Height: 4.8 inches

Width over grips: 1.37 inches

Length of barrel: 3.81 inches

Distance between front and rear sights: 4.88 inches

Unloaded weight: 23.3 oz.

Magazine capacity: 13 rounds

Bullet size: 90 grains (jacketed hollow point)

Muzzle velocity: 1000 ft/s

Energy: 200 ft/lbf

APPLICABLE NITA STATUTES

Nita Criminal Code, Chapter 40.

Section 18-3-101. Homicide, definition of terms.

4. Homicide means the killing of a person by another.

5. Person, when referring to the victim of a homicide, means a human being who had been born and was alive at the time of the homicidal act.

6. The term after deliberation means not only intentionally, but also that the decision to commit the act has been made after the exercise of reflection and judgment concerning the act. An act committed after deliberation is never one that has been committed in a hasty or impulsive manner.

Section 18-3-102. Murder in the first degree.

3. A person commits the crime of murder in the first degree if:

    a. After deliberation and with the intent to cause the death of a person other than himself, he causes the death of that person or of another person.

4. Murder in the first degree is a class 1 felony.

Section 18-3-103. Murder in the second degree.

4. A person commits the crime of murder in the second degree if:

    a. She intentionally, but not after deliberation, causes the death of a person; or

    b. With intent to cause serious bodily injury to a person other than herself, she causes the death of that person or of another person.

5. Diminished responsibility due to lack of mental capacity is not a defense to murder in the second degree.

6. Murder in the second degree is a class 2 felony.

Section 18-3-104. Manslaughter.

3. A person commits the crime of manslaughter if:

    a. He recklessly causes the death of a person; or

    b. He intentionally, but not after deliberation, causes the death of a person, under circumstances where the act causing the death was performed upon a sudden heat of passion caused by a serious and highly provoking act of the intended victim, affecting the person killing sufficiently to excite an irresistible passion in a reasonable person; but if between the provocation and the killing there is an interval sufficient for the voice of reason and humanity to be heard, the killing is murder.

4. Manslaughter is a class 4 felony.

Section 18-3-105. Criminally negligent homicide.

4. A person commits the crime of criminally negligent homicide if:

   a. By conduct amounting to criminal negligence, she causes the death of a person; or

   b. She intentionally causes the death of a person, but she believes in good faith that circumstances exist that would justify the act under §§ 18-1-701 and 18-1-702, but her belief that such circumstances exist is unreasonable.

5. Criminally negligent homicide is a class 1 misdemeanor.

Section 18-1-105. Felonies classified, penalties.

Felonies are divided into four classes that are distinguished from one another by the following penalties that are authorized upon conviction:

Class	Minimum Sentence	Maximum Sentence
1	50 years imprisonment	Life imprisonment
2	10 years imprisonment	50 years imprisonment
3	5 years imprisonment	40 years imprisonment
4	1 year imprisonment, or two thousand dollars fine	10 years imprisonment, or thirty thousand dollars fine, or

Section 18-1-106. Misdemeanors classified, penalties.

Misdemeanors are divided into three classes that are distinguished from one another by the following penalties that are authorized upon conviction:

Class	Minimum Sentence	Maximum Sentence
1	12 months imprisonment, or one thousand dollars fine, or both	24 months imprisonment, or five thousand dollars fine, or both
2	6 months imprisonment, or five hundred dollars fine, or both	12 months imprisonment, or one thousand dollars fine, or both
3	Fifty dollars fine	6 months imprisonment, or five hundred dollars fine, or both

No term of imprisonment for conviction of a misdemeanor shall be served in the state penitentiary unless served concurrently with a term for conviction of a felony.

Section 18-1-501. Principles of criminal culpability, definitions.

The following definitions are applicable to the determination of culpability requirements for offenses defined in this code:

10. Act means a bodily movement and includes words and possession of property.

11. Conduct means an act or omission and its accompanying state of mind or, where relevant, a series of acts or omissions.

12. Criminal negligence. A person acts with criminal negligence when, through a gross deviation from the standard of care that a reasonable person would exercise, he fails to perceive a substantial and unjustifiable risk that a result will occur or that a circumstance exists.

13. Culpable mental state means intentionally, or knowingly, or recklessly, or with criminal negligence as these terms are defined in this section.

14. Intentionally. A person acts intentionally with respect to a result or to a conduct described by a statute defining an offense when his conscious objective is to cause such result or to engage in such conduct.

15. Knowingly. A person acts knowingly with respect to conduct or to a circumstance described by a statute defining an offense when she is aware that her conduct is of such nature or that such circumstance exists.

16. Omission means a failure to perform an act to which a duty or performance is imposed by law.

17. Recklessly. A person acts recklessly when he consciously disregards a substantial and unjustifiable risk that a result will occur or that a circumstance exists.

18. Voluntary act means an act performed consciously as a result of effort or determination and includes the possession of property if the actor was aware of her physical possession or control thereof for a sufficient period to have been able to terminate it.

Sections 18-1-701 and 18-1-702. Justification and Exemption from Criminal Responsibility.

Section 18-1-701. Use of physical force, special relationship.

The use of physical force upon another person that would otherwise constitute an offense is justifiable and not criminal under any of the following circumstances:

* * *

6. A person acting under a reasonable belief that another person is about to commit suicide or to inflict serious physical injury upon himself may use reasonable and appropriate physical force upon that person to the extent that it is reasonably necessary to thwart the result.

Section 18-1-702. Use of physical force in defense of a person.

4. A person is justified in using physical force upon another person in order to defend herself or a third person from what she reasonably believes to be the use or imminent use of unlawful physical force by that other person, and she may use a degree of force that she reasonably believes to be necessary for that purpose.

5. Deadly physical force may be used only if a person reasonably believes a lesser degree of force is inadequate, and the actor has reasonable ground to believe, and does believe, that he or another person is in imminent danger of being killed or receiving great bodily harm.

6. Notwithstanding the provisions of subsection (1), a person is not justified in using physical force if:

    a. With intent to cause physical injury or death to another person, she provokes the use of unlawful physical force by that other person; or

b.   She is the initial aggressor; or

c.   The physical force involved is the product of a combat by agreement not specifically authorized by law.

Justification and Affirmative Defenses, Nita Supreme Court

State v. Pierizak, 78 Nita 2d 68 (YR-4). The criminal case law in Nita is well settled that for affirmative defenses involving principles of justification, the burden of proof is on the State. The defendant has the burden of going forward by raising the defense and presenting some evidence of the defense. But once that is done, the burden of proof is on the State to prove each element of the crime charged, including the issue raised by the defense of justification. The term "affirmative defense" is somewhat misleading because the burden is not on the defendant to prove the defense. Under § 18-1-606 of the Nita Criminal Code, once the issue of the defense is raised by "some evidence," the State "must sustain the burden of proving the defendant guilty beyond a reasonable doubt as to that issue together with all the other elements of the offense." *See also State v. Meninger*, 198 Nita 351 (YR-22).

Proposed Jury Instructions

The following jury instructions are intended for use with any of the files contained in these materials regardless of whether the trial is in Nita state court or in federal court. In addition, each of these files contains special instructions dealing with the law applicable in the particular case. The instructions set forth here state general principles that may be applicable in any of the cases and may be used at the discretion of the trial judge.*

Part I: Preliminary Instructions

(Given prior to the evidence.)

Nita Instruction 01:01. Introduction

You have been selected as jurors and have taken an oath to well and truly try this case. This trial will last one day.

During the progress of the trial there will be periods of time when the Court recesses. During those periods of time, you must not talk about this case among yourselves or with anyone else.

During the trial, do not talk to any of the parties, their lawyers, or any of the witnesses.

If any attempt is made by anyone to talk to you concerning the matters here under consideration, you should immediately report that fact to the Court.

You should keep an open mind. You should not form or express an opinion during the trial and should reach no conclusion in this case until you have heard all of the evidence, the arguments of counsel, and the final instructions as to the law that will be given to you by the Court.

Nita Instruction 01:02. Conduct of the Trial

First, the attorneys will have an opportunity to make opening statements. These statements are not evidence and should be considered only as a preview of what the attorneys expect the evidence will be.

Following the opening statements, witnesses will be called to testify. They will be placed under oath and questioned by the attorneys. Documents and other tangible exhibits may also be received as evidence. If an exhibit is given to you to examine, you should examine it carefully, individually, and without comment.

It is counsel's right and duty to object when testimony or other evidence is being offered that he believes is not admissible.

When the Court sustains an objection to a question, the jurors must disregard the question and the answer, if one has been given, and draw no inference from the question or answer or speculate as to what the witness would have said if permitted to answer. Jurors must also disregard evidence stricken from the record.

When the Court sustains an objection to any evidence, the jurors must disregard the evidence.

---

* The instructions contained in this section are borrowed or adapted from a number of sources, including California, Illinois, Indiana, Washington, and Colorado pattern jury instructions.

When the Court overrules an objection to any evidence, the jurors must not give that evidence any more weight than if the objection had not been made.

When the evidence is completed, the attorneys will make final statements. These final statements are not evidence, but are given to assist you in evaluating the evidence. The attorneys are also permitted to argue in an attempt to persuade you to a particular verdict. You may accept or reject those arguments as you see fit.

Finally, just before you retire to consider your verdict, I will give you further instructions on the law that applies to this case.

Part II: Final Instructions

(Given after the parties have rested.)

General Principles

Nita Instruction 2:01. Introduction

Members of the jury, the evidence and arguments in this case have been completed, and I will now instruct you as to the law.

The law applicable to this case is stated in these instructions, and it is your duty to follow all of the instructions. You must not single out certain instructions and disregard others.

It is your duty to determine the facts and to determine them only from the evidence in this case. You are to apply the law to the facts and in this way decide the case. You must not be governed or influenced by sympathy or prejudice for or against any party in this case. Your verdict must be based on evidence and not on speculation, guess, or conjecture.

From time to time the court has ruled on the admissibility of evidence. You must not concern yourselves with the reasons for these rulings. You should disregard questions and exhibits that were withdrawn or on which objections were sustained.

You should also disregard testimony and exhibits that the court has refused or stricken.

The evidence that you should consider consists only of the witnesses' testimonies and the exhibits the court has received.

Any evidence that was received for a limited purpose should not be considered by you for any other purpose.

You should consider all the evidence in the light of your own observations and experiences in life.

Neither by these instructions nor by any ruling or remark that I have made do I mean to indicate any opinion as to the facts or as to what your verdict should be.

Nita Instruction 2:02. Opening Statements and Closing Arguments

Opening statements are made by the attorneys to acquaint you with the facts they expect to prove. Closing arguments are made by the attorneys to discuss the facts and circumstances in the case and should be confined to the evidence and to reasonable inferences to be drawn therefrom. Neither opening statements nor closing arguments are evidence, and any statement or argument made by the attorneys that is not based on the evidence should be disregarded.

Nita Instruction 2:03. Credibility of Witnesses

You are the sole judges of the credibility of the witnesses and of the weight to be given to the testimony of each witness. In determining what credit is to be given any witness, you may take into account the witness's ability and opportunity to observe; the witness's manner and appearance while testifying; any interest, bias, or prejudice the witness may have; the reasonableness of the witness's testimony considered in light of all the evidence; and any other factors that bear on the believability and weight of the witness's testimony.

Nita Instruction 2:04. Expert Witnesses

You have heard evidence in this case from witnesses who testified as experts. The law allows experts to express an opinion on subjects involving their special knowledge, training and skill, experience, or research. While their opinions are allowed to be given, it is entirely within the province of the jury to determine what weight shall be given their testimony. Jurors are not bound by the testimony of experts; their testimony is to be weighed as that of any other witness.

Nita Instruction 2:05. Direct and Circumstantial Evidence

The law recognizes two kinds of evidence: direct and circumstantial. Direct evidence proves a fact directly; that is, the evidence by itself, if true, establishes the fact. Circumstantial evidence is the proof of facts or circumstances that give rise to a reasonable inference of other facts; that is, circumstantial evidence process a fact indirectly in that it follows from other facts or circumstances according to common experience and observations in life. An eyewitness is a common example of direct evidence while human footprints are circumstantial evidence that a person was present.

The law makes no distinction between direct and circumstantial evidence as to the degree or amount of proof required, and each should be considered according to whatever weight or value it may have. All of the evidence should be considered and evaluated by you in arriving at your verdict.

Nita Instruction 2:06. Concluding Instruction

I did not in any way, and do not by these instructions, give or intimate any opinions as to what has or has not been proven in the case, or as to what are or are not the facts of the case.

No one of these instructions states all of the law applicable, but all of them must be taken, read, and considered together as they are connected with and related to each other as a whole.

You must not be concerned with the wisdom of any rule of law. Regardless of any opinions you may have as to what the law ought to be, it would be a violation of your sworn duty to base a verdict on any other view of the law than that given in these instructions.

Nita Instruction 3:01. Indictment (Information)

The indictment in this case is the formal method of accusing the defendant of a crime and placing him on trial. It is not any evidence against the defendant and does not create any inference of guilt. The State has the burden of proving beyond a reasonable doubt every essential element of the crime charged in the indictment or any of the crimes included therein.

Nita Instruction 3:02. Burden of Proof

The State has the burden of proving the guilt of the defendant beyond a reasonable doubt, and this burden remains on the State throughout the case. The defendant is not required to prove his innocence.

Nita Instruction 3:03. Reasonable Doubt

Reasonable doubt means a doubt based on reason and common sense that arises from a fair and rational consideration of all the evidence or lack of evidence in the case. It is a doubt that is not a vague, speculative, or imaginary doubt, but such a doubt as would cause reasonable persons to hesitate to act in matters of importance to themselves.

Nita Instruction 3:04. Presumption of Innocence

The defendant is presumed to be innocent of the charges against him. This presumption remains with him throughout every stage of the trial and during your deliberations on the verdict. The presumption is not overcome until, from all the evidence in the case, you are convinced beyond a reasonable doubt that the defendant is guilty.

Nita Instruction 3:05. Reputation/Character

The defendant has introduced evidence of his character and reputation for (truth and veracity) (being a peaceful and law-abiding citizen) (morality) (chastity) (honesty and integrity) (etc.). This evidence may be sufficient when considered with the other evidence in the case to raise a reasonable doubt of the defendant's guilt. However, if from all the evidence in the case you are satisfied beyond a reasonable doubt of the defendant's guilt, then it is your duty to find him guilty, even though he may have a good reputation for_____.

CASE-SPECIFIC INSTRUCTIONS

1. The court will now instruct you on the law governing this case. You must arrive at your verdict by unanimous vote, applying the law, as you are now instructed, to the facts as you find them to be.

2. The State of Nita has charged the defendant, Trudi Doyle, with the crime of first-degree murder, which includes the crimes of second-degree murder, manslaughter, and criminally negligent homicide. The defendant has pleaded not guilty.

3. Under the criminal code of the State of Nita, a person commits the crime of first-degree murder if, after deliberation and with the intent to cause the death of a person other than himself, he causes the death of that person or of another person.

   Person, when referring to the victim of a homicide, means a human being who had been born and was alive at the time of the homicidal act.

   After deliberation means not only intentionally, but also that the decision to commit the act has been made after the exercise of reflection and judgment concerning the act. An act committed after deliberation is never one that has been committed in a hasty or impulsive manner.

4. Under the criminal code of the State of Nita, a person commits the crime of second-degree murder if,

   a. He intentionally, but not after deliberation, causes the death of another person; or

   b. With intent to cause serious injury to a person other than himself, he causes the death of that person.

   Intentionally. A person acts intentionally with respect to a result or to conduct described by a statute defining a crime when his conscious objective is to cause such result or to engage in such conduct.

5. Under the criminal code of the State of Nita, a person commits the crime of manslaughter if,

   a. He recklessly causes the death of a person; or

   b. He intentionally, but not after deliberation, causes the death of a person, under circumstances where the act causing the death was performed upon a sudden heat of passion caused by a serious and highly provoking act of the intended victim, but if between the provocation and the killing there is an interval sufficient for the voice of reason and humanity to be heard, the killing is murder.

   Recklessly. A person acts recklessly when he consciously disregards a substantial and unjustifiable risk that a result will occur or that a circumstance exists.

6. Under the criminal code of the State of Nita, a person commits the crime of criminally negligent homicide if,

   a. By conduct amounting to criminal negligence he causes the death of a person; or

   b. He intentionally causes the death of a person, but he believes in good faith that circumstances exist that would justify his conduct, but his belief that such circumstances exist is unreasonable.

Conduct means an act or omission and its accompanying state of mind, or a series of acts or omissions.

Criminal negligence. A person acts with criminal negligence when through a gross deviation from the standard of care that a reasonable person would exercise, he fails to perceive a substantial and unjustifiable risk that a result will occur or that a circumstance exists.

7. The use of physical force on another person is justifiable and not criminal when a person acts under a reasonable belief that another person is about to commit suicide or to inflict serious bodily injury upon herself and he uses reasonable and appropriate physical force upon that person to the extent that it is reasonably necessary to thwart the result.

8. A person is justified in using physical force upon another person in order to defend himself or a third person from what he reasonably believes to be the use or imminent use of unlawful physical force by that other person, and he may use a degree of force that he reasonably believes to be necessary for that purpose.

    However, deadly physical force upon another person may be used only if a person reasonably believes a lesser degree of force is inadequate and the actor has reasonable ground to believe, and does believe, that he or another person is in imminent danger of being killed or of receiving great bodily harm.

9. To sustain the charge of first-degree murder, the state must prove the following propositions:

    a. That the defendant performed the acts that caused the death of Johnny Diamond, a human being; and

    b. That defendant acted after deliberation and with the intent to cause the death of Johnny Diamond or any other person.

    If you find from your consideration of all the evidence that each of these propositions has been proved beyond a reasonable doubt, then you should find the defendant guilty of first-degree murder.

    If, on the other hand, you find from your consideration of all the evidence that either of these propositions has not been proved beyond a reasonable doubt, then you should find the defendant not guilty of first-degree murder.

10. To sustain the charge of second-degree murder, the State must prove the following propositions:

    a. That the defendant performed the acts that caused the death of Johnny Diamond, a human being; and

    b. The defendant intended to kill or cause serious bodily injury to Johnny Diamond; and

    c. That the defendant was not justified in using the force that she used.

    If you find from your consideration of all the evidence that each of these propositions has been proved beyond a reasonable doubt, then you should find the defendant guilty of second-degree murder.

    If, on the other hand, you find from your consideration of all the evidence that any of these propositions has not been proved beyond a reasonable doubt, then you should find the defendant not guilty of second-degree murder.

11. To sustain the charge of manslaughter, the State must prove the following propositions:

    a. That the defendant performed the acts that caused the death of Johnny Diamond, a human being; and

    b. That the defendant acted recklessly; or she acted intentionally, but under a sudden heat of passion caused by a serious and highly provoking action by Johnny Diamond.

    If you find from your consideration of all the evidence that each of these propositions has been proved beyond a reasonable doubt, then you should find the defendant guilty of manslaughter.

    If, on the other hand, you find from your consideration of all the evidence that either of these propositions has not been proved beyond a reasonable doubt, then you should find the defendant not guilty of manslaughter.

12. To sustain the charge of criminally negligent homicide, the State must prove the following propositions:

    a. That the defendant performed the acts that caused the death of Johnny Diamond, a human being; and

    b. That the defendant acted with criminal negligence; or he acted intentionally, but believed in good faith that circumstances existed that would have justified the killing of Johnny Diamond, and the defendant's belief that such circumstances existed was unreasonable.

    If you find from your consideration of all the evidence that each of these propositions has been proved beyond a reasonable doubt, then you should find the defendant guilty of criminally negligent homicide.

    If, on the other hand, you find from your consideration of all the evidence that either of these propositions has not been proved beyond a reasonable doubt, then you should find the defendant not guilty of criminally negligent homicide.

13. The unintentional killing of a human being is excusable and not unlawful when committed by accident in the performance of a lawful act by lawful means and where the person causing the death acted with that care and caution that would be exercised by an ordinarily careful and prudent individual under like circumstances.

    If you find that Johnny Diamond lost his life by such an accident, then you should find the defendant not guilty.

14. When a person commits an act by accident under circumstances that show no evil design, intention, or culpable negligence, he does not thereby commit a crime.

    If you find that Johnny Diamond lost his life by such an accident, then you should find the defendant not guilty.

IN THE CIRCUIT COURT OF
DARROW COUNTY, NITA

THE PEOPLE OF THE STATE OF NITA	)	
	)	
v.	)	Case No. CR2216
	)	
TRUDI DOYLE,	)	JURY VERDICT
Defendant.	)	

We, the Jury, return the following verdict, and each of us concurs in this verdict: [Choose the appropriate verdict]

NOT GUILTY

We, the Jury, find the defendant, Trudi Doyle, NOT GUILTY.

_____

Foreperson

OR
FIRST-DEGREE MURDER

We, the Jury, find the defendant, Trudi Doyle, GUILTY of Murder in the First Degree.

_____

Foreperson

OR
SECOND-DEGREE MURDER

We, the Jury, find the defendant, Trudi Doyle, GUILTY of Murder in the Second Degree.

_____

Foreperson

OR
MANSLAUGHTER

We, the Jury, find the defendant, Trudi Doyle, GUILTY of Manslaughter.

_____

Foreperson

OR
CRIMINALLY NEGLIGENT HOMICIDE

We, the Jury, find the defendant, Trudi Doyle, GUILTY of Criminally Negligent Homicide.

_____

Foreperson